ESSAYS ON SOCIALISM

ESSAYS ON SOCIALISM

ANNIE BESANT

GYAN

Published by

GYAN

Gyan Publishing House
5, Ansari Road
Daryaganj, New Delhi-110002
Phone: 011-47034999, 9811692060
E-mail: books@gyanbooks.com

Distribution Network
gyanbooks.com
India, USA, Canada, UK, Australia

ISBN: 978-93-6780-279-3 (PB)
First Published, 1887

2nd Impression 2024

Printed at: Gyan Press, Delhi.

ESSAYS ON SOCIALISM
Author: ANNIE BESANT

ESSAYS ON SOCIALISM

BY

ANNIE BESANT

Price Two Shillings and Sixpence.

LONDON
ROBERT FORDER, 28 STONECUTTER ST., E.C.
1893

Contents.

THE REDISTRIBUTION OF POLITICAL POWER.

BY

ANNIE BESANT.

LONDON:
FREETHOUGHT PUBLISHING COMPANY,
63, FLEET STREET, E.C.
1885.

PRICE FOURPENCE

THE REDISTRIBUTION OF POLITICAL POWER.

RESULTS OF THE REFORM BILL OF 1832.

STANDING as we do face to face with the enfranchisement of two million men and the redistribution of electoral power in the community, it seems well to look back on earlier Reform Bills and to endeavor to judge of the probable results of the present measures from the results that have followed their predecessors. My object in the following pages is to trace out the most important tendencies which have shown themselves after each Reform Bill; to mark the chief activities manifested after each "infusion of new blood"; to present a picture of certain steadily developing modifications of the national organism, modifications which are likely to become very pronounced in the near future. I am not aware that any attempt has been made to distinguish the transitory from the permanent tendencies, the reforms done once for all amid great excitement from the apparently less important measures which none the less initiate new eras and serve as the starting-point for new developments. Yet in sociology as in geology, the most far-reaching changes are not made by the volcanoes and the earthquakes, but by the slow action of countless silent ever-working forces.

Each Reform Bill has been followed by a great outburst of reforming energy, and amid the many measures carried in the reformed Parliaments those are, I think, of the most permanently important character which have dealt with the conditions of Labor, with the extension of Religious Liberty and Equality, with the Tenure of Land, with the Education of the People.

One marked change has come over the nation apart from any legislative enactment—the decrease of the power of the hereditary peers after each Reform Bill. That of '32 swept away from them their control of the House of Commons; after '67, their legislative chamber became less and less able to hold its own against the increased power of the popular representatives; on the Bill of '84 they nearly shipwrecked their House, and when the new constituencies have had their say we may hope that the abolition of their hereditary right of obstruction will be within measurable distance.

We shall not be able to estimate the changes brought about after 1832 without glancing at the England of the pre-reforming period. The power of the great houses then controlled the elections of so many boroughs that the peers practically made the government; in the list given by Lord John Russell in 1831, we find boroughs returning members in which the constituencies consisted of 13, 18, 5, 10, 12, persons, and in one case of no persons at all. In these dukes, marquises, earls, and great untitled commoners, appointed whom they would as the members to serve in Parliament. Molesworth says: "In most of these boroughs the seats were sold by the proprietors. Sometimes they themselves or some of their relatives or dependents were nominated to represent them. Bribery was also practised with little or no reserve or concealment where it was necessary, but in many instances the constituency was so dependent on the proprietor that no expenditure of this kind was requisite" (History of the Reform Bill, page 116). Lord John Russell urged that a stranger visiting the country "would be very much astonished if he were taken to a ruined mound, and told that the mound sent two representatives to Parliament—if he were taken to a stone wall, and told that three niches in it sent two representatives to Parliament—if he were taken to a park, where no houses were to be seen, and told that that park sent two representatives to Parliament" (Ibid., p. 104).

Complaints of a similar nature were put even more forcibly in a petition presented to the House of Commons as early as 1793, in which the petitioners stated that "seventy of your honorable members are returned by thirty-five places, where the right of voting is vested in burgage and other tenures of a similar description, and in which it would be to trifle with the patience of your honorable house to mention any number of voters whatever, the elections at the places alluded to being notoriously a mere matter of form"; further that two hundred and twenty more were elected by places in which the electors varied from less than fifty to less than two hundred; that one hundred and fifty-seven members were sent to Parliament by the direct authority of eighty-four individuals, and one hundred and fifty more "not by the collective voice of those they appear to represent, but by the recommendation of seventy powerful individuals", one hundred and fifty persons thus returning a majority of the House (Ibid., pp. 342, 343, 347).

The agitation outside against this intolerable political condition was sharpened by poverty and distress among the people. Then, as now, social suffering was widespread and alarming. The Non-intercourse Act, passed by the United States, shut the American market against England, while the introduction of machinery into various manufactures threw numbers of persons out of employment, and the year 1811 was marked by the "Luddite riots", in which the new and hated machines were destroyed by the infuriated workers. But these, isolated by ignorance, could enter into no effective and organised action for their own good; they could make riots, they could burn a castle; they could not formulate their demands and enforce them. In 1819, at Peterloo, the savage yeomanry rode at the helpless crowd, cutting with their swords in every direction, till six hundred and eighteen people were wounded and fourteen were killed. (See Hunt's speech, reported in "Molesworth", p. 126.) But the answer to this was not Reform, but the infamous "Six Acts" of Lord Sidmouth, generally called "Castlereagh's Six Acts", which gave more speedy execution of justice in certain cases, prevented unauthorised military training, punished so-called "libels", gave authority to seize arms, forbad "seditious" meetings, and imposed a stamp duty.

Even when at last a Reform Bill was introduced, it met with bitter opposition. Sir Charles Wetherell railed against it in the true Tory style, prophesying all sorts of mischiefs as the consequences of Reform. "I say that the principle of the Bill is Republican at the basis; I say that it is destructive of all property, of all right, of all privilege; and that the same arbitrary violence which expelled a majority of members from that House at the time of the Commonwealth, is now, after the lapse of a century from the Revolution, during which the population has enjoyed greater happiness than has been enjoyed by any population under heaven, proceeding to expose the House of Commons again to the nauseous experiment of a repetition of Pride's purge" (Ibid., p. 132). Spite of all these terrible forebodings the Bill passed into law, receiving the Royal Assent on June 7th, 1832.

The general result of the Act was to throw political power into the hands of manufacturers and capitalists, in a phrase to "enfranchise the middle classes". The direct influence of the working classes was, if anything, slightly diminished by the Act, since it disfranchised a few places in which they had previously possessed the suffrage. It struck a fatal blow at the privileges of the possessors of hereditary authority, and gave representation to the commercial interests of the nation. One striking proof was given that the class which then won political power was not unworthy of the freedom it had gained. One of its first reforms was the introduction of a Factory Act to protect the more helpless of the operative class, and it ought never to be forgotten that effective legislative interference with employers was due to a Parliament elected principally by that very same *bourgeois* class which it is now the fashion to so unsparingly denounce.

In 1801 the first Act limiting the hours of labor was passed, and by this it was forbidden that apprentices should work for more than twelve hours a day; in 1819 Sir Robert Peel was defeated in a Bill which proposed to limit the working day for young persons under sixteen years of age to eleven hours and a half, and the Act of 1801 appears to have been systematically evaded. When the Reformed Parliament met in 1833, a Bill was introduced in the preamble of which it was stated that "it has become a practice to employ a great number of children and young persons of both sexes an unreasonable length of time, and late at night, and in many cases all night";

this Bill enacted that no child should be employed in any factory or mill (except a silk manufactory) under ten years of age, and limited the working day to nine hours for children under fourteen. In silk mills children under the age of thirteen were still allowed to work for ten hours a day. The hours of labor for young persons over fourteen and under eighteen were fixed at sixty-nine a week or eleven-and-a-half a day. Inspectors were also appointed to see to the proper carrying out of the law, but it was nevertheless evaded, and in 1838 Lord Ashley proposed another measure for the protection of children, but his Bill was thrown out by 121 votes against 106. In 1842, the same gentleman successfully carried through a Bill prohibiting the employment of women and children in coal mines, and thus put a stop to the torture of young children, and to the wholesale demoralisation which accompanied the working together of men and women stripped to the waist in the mines. Lord Londonderry, as a large coal-owner, bitterly opposed the Bill, affording one more example of the fact that "humanity" vanishes before the greed for wealth, and that the life and happiness of the employed weigh little when put in the balances against increased profit for the employer. In 1844 an unsuccessful attempt to limit the working of women and children in factories to a Ten Hours' Day, brought in by Lord Ashley, was opposed by the Government and was defeated, and a similar fate befell the same measure when re-introduced in 1846 by Mr. Fielden. In 1847, however, Mr. Fielden carried a bill reducing the working day to ten hours for young persons up to the age of eighteen.

This group of measures, passed by the Reformed Parliaments, may be taken as laying down the principle of legislative interference between employers and employed, of protecting the latter by law against the former. That this principle will, in time to come, be carried considerably further is, to my mind, not a matter of doubt, and those who object to further legislation in the interests of labor ought in consistency to advocate the repeal of all the laws on that matter already passed. They should send back women to work half naked in the coal-mines. They should bid the young children leave the schoolroom and the playground, and go back to the factory to toil all day "and late at night and in many cases all night", till they fall asleep over their work, and till, lying at home on their pallets, their little hands in sleep still toss the shuttle to and fro.[1] They should call on the law to stand aside and to let the wild struggle for life go on unchecked. They should allow the workers to trample each other down in the fearful competition for bread, and the employers to wring from their necessities the greatest amount of labor at the lowest wage. So shall the sacred "freedom of contract" remain untouched, and the beautiful spectacle of anarchical competition unrestrained by law shall be offered as the outcome of civilization. Wild beasts rend each other in their strife over the carcase of their prey; why not men in their strife for bread and wealth?

With regard to Religious Liberty the Reformed Parliaments made vast changes between 1833 and 1867. In 1833 a Bill for abolishing the civil disabilities of the Jews was passed by the House of Commons but rejected by the Lords, and thus began the long struggle which ended only in 1860 by the Act which abolished the Christian oath for members of Parliament. In 1834 the Commons passed Bills for the abolition of University Tests, for the abolition

---

[1] *From Evidence from the Report of the Committee of the House of Lords,* 1819.—*T. Wilkinson.*—"What are the hours of working in the factories you are acquainted with?—From six to seven in the summer, and from seven to eight in the winter. What time is allowed for dinner?—An hour. Is any other time allowed for meals?—No. Are the children ever obliged to be at the factory before or after the common hours of work?—Yes. Are they ever beaten to make them work?—I have seen hundreds beat, to keep them awake and drive them on." *John Farebrother.*—"How old were you when you first went in?—Between five and six. When the children have to eat their meals in the factory, do they generally finish it?—No. Do they leave much of it?—Yes; I have seen it all left many times. Is that owing to its being covered with dust?—Yes. How do they get their breakfast and afternoon meal?—As they can catch it; when the machinery is moving they eat it as they are piecing. How soon do you begin to see a difference in a child's health?—I have seen a difference in one week." *Evidence before the House of Commons Committee in* 1816.—*J. Moss.* "He had on one occasion known children to work in the mill from eight o'clock on Saturday night to six on Sunday morning. The same children resumed work on Sunday night at twelve o'clock, and worked until five in the morning. . . . He had known children to work for three weeks together from five in the morning till nine or ten at night, with the exception of one hour for meals; he had frequently found the children asleep on the mill floors, after the time they should have been in bed."

of Church Rates, for allowing marriages in Dissenters' chapels, but all these were rejected by the Lords, the struggle over University Tests lasting until 1871, after a second Reform Act. In 1836, the right of registering births, marriages, and deaths was taken from the clergy of the Established Church, and in the same year a Bill was passed permitting Dissenters to be married in their own chapels. In 1837 an attempt was made to relieve Dissenters from the payment of Church Rates, but the Bill was withdrawn in consequence of the opposition raised to it, and the measure was not carried until 1868, after the impulse of a new Reform. In 1840 a small instalment of justice to Ireland in religious matters was made by the Irish Tithe Bill, which had been originally introduced in 1834, and rejected in 1835, 1836, and 1837; in 1857 another small instalment was paid by the abolition of a tax called "Ministers' Money" which had been levied for the support of the Establishment. The great agitation for the disestablishment of the Irish Church was commenced in Parliament by Mr. Dillwyn in 1865; it was endorsed by the Liberal Party in Mr. Gladstone's famous resolutions for disestablishing and disendowing it, carried in the unreformed Parliament in March 1868, and the way was thus opened for a Bill on the subject after the general election. The claim of Dissenters to be allowed to bury their dead without the intrusion of the State-paid priests went too far on the path of religious equality for the Parliaments between 1833 and 1867; the establishment of cemeteries whereof a part remained unconsecrated for their use was permitted, but complete freedom of burial was only obtained by them in 1880, and this is not even yet extended to thorough-going heretics.

With respect to the Tenure of Land, nothing of any importance to the nation was done between 1832 and 1867. A number of bills affecting land were passed, but they were all on points touching only the landowners, and nothing was even suggested which could imply that the nation had the smallest interest in its own soil. The great Corn Law struggle, which ended with the passing of the Anti-Corn Law Bill in 1846, was, however, really a struggle between the masses of the people wanting cheap bread and the landlords wanting to keep out foreign corn; only by protection could farmers, they thought, continue to pay high rents for the land they cultivated, and the "protection of agriculture" then, as now, was nothing more than an attempt on the part of the landlords to tax the community for their own benefit. Here, as everywhere else, the interests of the small land-monopolising class were in direct conflict with the interests of the masses of the people. The people need cheap food; the landlords want food to be dear, so that the farmers who supply it may be able to pay high rent; every attempt to keep out foreign corn, foreign cattle, foreign food of any kind, is an attempt to maintain unfair rents by forcing up the prices of farmers' produce, and to levy a tax on the consumers for the maintenance of an evil system.

The roots of our present system of National Education are struck in the first Parliament after the Reform Act of 1832. In 1833 a grant of £20,000 a year was made for the purposes of National Education, but it was placed for administration in the hands of the National Society and of the British and Foreign School Society; so that although the grant implied a recognition of the duty of the community towards its children, the recognition took the unhealthy form of placing State funds in the hands of unofficial societies. Practically most of the money was disposed of by the clergy, and was used for denominational purposes. In 1839 the grant was raised to £30,000 a-year, and an Educational Committee of the Privy Council was appointed to receive and administer the money: this was the foundation of State Education, for not only was the money kept under State control, but inspectors were appointed over the schools assisted by the State, and so began the system which received such vast development after the Reform Bill of 1867, and which is likely to develop yet further in the near future. Those who oppose its development are bound in reason to object to the recognition of the whole principle of State Education, and to agitate for the abolition of the huge system which has grown out of the seeds planted in 1833 and 1839. Those who would leave education to "voluntary effort" should see what was its condition before the State stepped in on behalf of its helpless children, and should gravely ask themselves whether they really desire that the ignorance of the early part of the nineteenth century should return to shroud its close, and that the children of the twentieth century should be robbed of the knowledge which is raising the children of to-day.

While Parliament was thus laying the basis of a system of National Education for children, the yearning of the workers outside for wider knowledge forced on it other legislation, which was also essentially educational. This yearning took the form of a resolute agitation for an unstamped press, for the fourpenny stamp imposed on all newspapers placed them entirely out of the reach of the poorer workers. Never was a struggle for a noble object carried on with more resolute heroism, with more strenuous patience. It was waged almost entirely by the poor, men and women selling unstamped papers, going to gaol, and continuing the sale on their release. Glancing over the list of those prosecuted in the year ending September, 1834, I see a few well-known names, and many to me unknown. There are Henry Hetherington, John Cleave, James Watson, all prominent men; but few know Edmund Wastneys of Newcastle, Isabella Rose of Southampton, Richard Lee and Edmund Stallwood of Holborn, John Smith of the Strand, George Baker of Worcester, Edmund Somerside of Winlaton, W. Nicholls of Tottenham Court Road, Patrick Bready and Edward Gleave of Sheffield, John Chappell of Clifton, James Guest, Richard Jenkinson, Julius Faulkner, William Plastans, William Guest, Thomas Watts, all of Birmingham, Alexander Yates of Coventry; yet all these suffered imprisonment for the crime of selling unstamped newspapers. And so I might go on with list after list of these, the privates in Liberty's army, who were struck down in the battle, who by their sufferings won for us our freedom, and on whose unknown graves we cannot even lay a leaf of memory and of thanks.

In 1836 the stamp was reduced from 4d. to 1d., despite the argument that the reduction would "introduce a cheap and profligate press, one of the greatest curses that can be inflicted on humanity". This penny duty was levied on papers containing "news", or remarks on news, published periodically at intervals of less than twenty-six days, and "published for sale for a less price than sixpence, exclusive of the duty" (6th and 7th William IV., cap. 76, quoted in the Report of the Select Committee on Newspaper Stamps, 1851, p. iv.). The agitation continued against the 1d. stamp, and the Committee of 1851 reported against it because of "the impediments which it throws in the way of the diffusion of useful knowledge regarding current and recent events among the poorer classes" (Report, p. xii.). The stamp was abolished in 1855.

In 1860, Mr. Gladstone proposed and carried in the House of Commons a clause in his Budget Bill repealing the paper duties, so as to still further cheapen literature, but the Lords struck out the clause by a majority of 89. In 1861, however, Mr. Gladstone made the repeal a part of his financial measure in such fashion that the Lords would have been obliged to reject the Budget if they rejected the repeal clause, and as they did not venture on so dangerous an aggression the "taxes on knowledge" were taken off.

Of all the work done by the Reformed Parliaments that connected with education was perhaps the most vitally important and the most far-reaching. Without a cheap press, political education is impossible for the masses, and without political education reforms are either unattainable or inoperative. Education is the lever whereby political and social inequality shall be overturned, and with this lever in one hand and the trowel of political power in the other, Democracy will be armed to overturn the Wrong and to build up the Right.

II.—Results of the Reform Bill of 1867.

The question of Parliamentary Reform again took definite shape in 1858, after the convulsions caused by the Crimean War and the Indian Mutiny. In that year, the Tories being in power, Mr. John Bright formulated a new scheme of Reform, which proposed to give the franchise to all who paid the poor-rate in boroughs, to all who paid a £10 rental in counties, and to lodgers paying a similar rental. Voting by ballot was also adopted by the Reformers, for the protection of the poorer voters who were subjected to intimidation by their employers. In 1859 Mr. Disraeli introduced a Reform Bill containing a most extraordinary collection of fancy property franchises, and on this the Government was defeated, and Lord Derby went to the country. After the general election Lord Palmerston came into power, and in the following year, 1860, Lord John Russell introduced a measure which gave a £6 franchise in boroughs, and a £10 in counties; in this Bill appeared for the first time the proposal to make "three-cornered constituencies", in which a minority might secure representation by electing one member out of three. The Bill made but slow progress in the House, and excited no enthusiasm out-of-doors, and it was finally withdrawn by the Government on June 11th. The question of Reform then slept until 1865, when Mr. Baines brought up some resolutions in its favor, and the Government declined to take any action in the matter; the feeling outside had, however, been growing steadily, and after the general election of 1865—in which Mr. Gladstone was defeated at Oxford and returned for South Lancashire—the Liberal party found itself stronger than ever. On the assembling of Parliament, Earl Russell being Premier, Parliamentary Reform found a place in the Queen's speech, and Mr. Gladstone introduced the Government Bill on March 13th; the proposed was by no means a Radical one, the county franchise being fixed at £14, and the borough at £10, but the famous "Cave of Adullam" was formed against it, and the Whigs and Tories together defeated the Government. Lord Derby took office at the end of June, and the agitation in favor of Reform now rose to fever heat; the Government tried at first to coerce the people, but succeeded only in irritating them, as when it closed the gates of Hyde Park against a meeting of the Reform League, and a new way was made into the Park over the pulled-down railings. On this the Government decided to yield to the popular demand, and in March, 1867, Mr. Disraeli, after bringing forward some abortive resolutions, startled Whigs, Tories, Liberals, and Radicals by introducing his famous Reform Bill which gave household suffrage to ratepayers in the boroughs, and reduced the county franchise to a £15 qualification. The latter was further reduced to £10, and householders who paid their rates in their rents received also the franchise. The Bill, characterised by Lord Derby as "a leap in the dark", passed the House of Lords in August, and thus the second great Reform Bill of the century became law, the working classes in the towns winning their enfranchisement and becoming, so far as the boroughs were concerned, the real depositories of political power.

It was manifestly impossible for the Tories long to delay the appeal to the new electorate, working, as they were, with a minority in the House of Commons. Lord Derby resigned office, and was succeeded by Mr. Disraeli, at the beginning of the Session of 1868, and the opening of a new period of reforming energy was announced in the famous resolutions of Mr. Gladstone, carried by a majority of 66, proposing to disestablish and disendow the Irish Church. Parliament was dissolved and a general election took place in November, resulting in the return of a large Liberal majority to the House of Commons. Mr. Gladstone, who in 1865 had proved too Liberal for Oxford, was in 1868 proved to be too Liberal for the county constituency of South Lancashire, but was returned by the working men of Greenwich, and became Premier of the new Liberal Ministry.

The Labor legislation of the period between the Reform Bills of 1867 and 1884 continued steadily on the lines laid down in the preceding period, and though fewer in number the Bills introduced were of the most valuable kind. In 1871 the Trade Union Act was passed, by which were repealed the iniquitous laws against combinations of workers. The law of 39 and 40 George III., cap. 106, to take an example of past legislation, punished combination by imprisonment, and rendered illegal all agreements between workmen for obtaining any advance of wages. Various Acts had been passed from time to time, partly repealing, partially re-enacting, this and similar oppressive measures, and the common law of conspiracy was constantly used against the Trades' Unions, the most outrageous sentences of penal servitude being passed on men under this law for combination and picketing. The natural result of oppression, secret outrages, appeared in many large towns; a strong agitation was carried on, and various Select Committees were appointed to consider the laws affecting the relations between employers and employed. The result was the passing of the Trade Union Act, which rendered the associations legal. This emancipating legislation was completed by the Employers and Workmen Bill, passed by Mr. Disraeli's Government in 1875, an Act which repealed all the oppressive penal laws under which labor had been so long suffering.

This same year 1875 was noticeable for the passing of the Artisans' Dwellings Bill, a well-meant measure, but which has proved inoperative, in consequence of its being permissive. A Shipping Bill, due to Mr. Plimsoll, was also passed during this year, and did something, though but little, to protect sailors' lives.

In 1874 a Bill introduced by Mr. Mundella, for extending the operation of the Factory Acts, had been taken up by the Government and passed; and in 1878 Mr. Cross succeeded in carrying another Bill, which had also been previously proposed by Mr. Mundella, for the consolidation and amendment of the Factory and Workshops Acts. This Act insisted on a sanitary condition for factories and workshops, and on the safeguarding of machinery; it limited the hours of labor for children, young persons, and women, prohibited the employment of children under ten years of age, provided for the education of child employees, set apart certain holidays and half-holidays, and required certificates of fitness for employment for children under sixteen years of age. On the whole the measure was a good one, though permitting too long hours of labor.

The Employers' Liability Bill of 1880, earnestly pleaded for by the representatives of labor in the House, made another important step forwards, by declaring that the employer might be made responsible for injuries received by his employees where such injury resulted from neglect by himself or by his agents.

Looking at the whole of this legislation, we find recognised as a definite principle the right of the community to interfere, by means of law, for the protection of the workers from the greed of those who employ them, whether it be to save sailors from "coffin-ships", or miners and other operatives from preventible injury, or factory and shop-workers from excessive hours of labor. We also find that the community recognises its interest in the wholesome housing of its laboring class, in the health of those producers on whom the wealth of the nation depends.

Some of the greatest blows struck for Religious Liberty and Equality during the century were dealt between 1867 and 1884. It is mentioned above that in 1868 Mr. Gladstone's resolutions against the Irish Establishment were carried in the unreformed Parliament by a majority of 66, and when Mr. Gladstone came into power as a result of the general election, the Liberal party was thereby pledged to attack the Irish Church without delay. On March 1st, 1869, Mr. Gladstone introduced a Bill for the

Disestablishment and Disendowment of the Irish Church. As the Church of the landlords and of a very small minority of the population, and as a badge of conquest, the Irish Church was quite peculiarly indefensible, yet it is needless to say that the Tory party loudly denounced the Bill as sacrilegious and confiscatory. It passed the Commons in May, but was returned to them so altered that they declined to accept it; after much wrangling the usual compromise was effected, and the Bill received the Royal Assent on July 26th. The great blunder of the Act lay in its clauses for compensating the officials of the defunct Establishment. Every official—including schoolmasters, clerks, and sextons —who was in office on January 1st, 1871, was declared to be entitled to payment of the net income which he was previously receiving so long as he discharged his office, such income to be further commutable for a capital sum, calculable on the value of the income as a life-annuity. The consequence of giving a seventeen months' period during which fresh interests could be created was, of course, to add largely to the class which had to be compensated, and so to diminish the funds applicable to national purposes. But the Act is of utmost value, in that it declared that the "ultimate surplus" was available for "the relief of unavoidable calamity and suffering", and that "the said proceeds shall be so applied accordingly, in the manner Parliament shall hereafter direct". That is, it laid down the precedent of treating the Church merely as a department of the State, the funds administered by which were national funds, to be used as the nation may direct.

The same year 1869 saw the passing of the Evidence Amendment Act, allowing witnesses without religious opinions to affirm in courts of law. As first introduced by the Hon. George Denman, it only permitted affirmation to those who should "object to take an oath". Charles Bradlaugh, now junior member for Northampton, pointed out that this would not enable Atheists to affirm, since they had been held "incompetent" to swear, whether they objected or not, and after some insistance a modification was made which authorised the taking of an affirmation by anyone who should "object to take an oath", or who should be objected to as "incompetent to take the oath". Unhappily the insulting words were added that the presiding judge must be "satisfied that the taking of an oath would have no binding effect on his conscience". This phrase has been constantly used as though Atheists stated that the oath was not binding on them, whereas the words were merely words of insult used by a Parliament in which Christians were in a large majority. The Evidence Further Amendment Act, passed in the following year, only extended the meaning of the word "judge" to "include any person or persons having by law authority to administer an oath for the taking of evidence". This Act was passed in consequence of the rejection of Mr. Bradlaugh's evidence by an arbitrator, the Court of Common Pleas holding that the evidence was rightly rejected, the Act of 1869 only admitting evidence given in a court of justice before a judge.

Since 1880, in consequence of Mr. Charles Bradlaugh's claim to affirm as a member of the House of Commons, various attempts have been made to legalise affirmation in Parliament. In June 1882 Lord Sundridge introduced a Bill permitting any member of either House to affirm if he intimated in writing that he had "a conscientious objection to the form of the oath required by the law, or that the taking of an oath would have no binding effect on his conscience". Objection was raised that the Government ought to deal with the matter rather than a private member, and the Bill failed to pass. In February, 1883, the Government introduced a similar Bill, but instead of making the conditions above stated, proposed that every member "may, if he thinks fit," affirm instead of swearing. The Government foolishly did not make their Bill a cabinet question, and it was lost by a majority of only three votes, proving that the least energy on their part would have ensured its success. In February, 1885, Mr. Hopwood, Q.C., introduced a far better measure, legalising affirmation "in all places and for all purposes where an oath is or shall be required by law". The fate of this new attempt to widen religious liberty is still doubtful when I write.

In 1871, the University Tests Bill, abolishing religious tests in the Universities, was at last passed, bitterly opposed as it was by the Tories, who denounced it in unmeasured terms; and by this funds usurped by the Church were rendered available for the education of Churchmen and of Dissenters alike. An attempt to do a similar service for Ireland, by the creation of a University from which theology should be excluded, was made by Mr. Gladstone in 1873, but this Bill was rejected by a majority of three. A Bill was, however, passed in this year abolishing tests in Trinity College, Dublin, and so a small step towards equality was made. In 1877, a Burial Acts Consolidation Bill was introduced in the House of Lords, which permitted "silent burial" in churchyards by Dissenters; but it was ultimately withdrawn, and quarrels over the coffins of dead Dissenters continued until 1880, in which year a Burials Bill was passed which permitted dissenting ministers to bury members of their sects in parish churchyards with any "religious and orderly service" they preferred. A strong effort was made to include all orderly forms of burial, Mr. Ashton Dilke pointing out that as he had no "religious" opinions the permission would not include himself, but the Christian majority was too intolerant to extend to extreme heretics the liberty it claimed for its own members, and an amending Burials Act is still required. It may be noted in passing that in 1879 Mr. Martin succeeded in passing through Parliament a Bill which made it incumbent on local authorities to provide cemeteries for the burial of Dissenters.

The prosecutions in 1883 of Messrs. Bradlaugh, Foote, Ramsey, and Kemp, for blasphemy, the conviction of the three latter, and the brutal sentences passed on them by Mr. Justice North, roused public feeling strongly against the Blasphemy Laws, and a Bill for their repeal was drafted by Mr. Justice Stephens. No member of the House of Commons, however, could be found bold enough to introduce it, and the abolition of these cruel laws is left to a more enlightened Parliament, chosen by a wider electorate.

Enormous progress was made in questions affecting the Tenure of Land between 1867 and 1884. First in order and in far-reaching importance comes Mr. Gladstone's great measure, the Irish Land Act. It was introduced in the Commons on February 15th, 1870, and became law on August 1st. By this Act the right of a tenant to his own improvements was recognised, and an attempt was made to prevent the confiscation by the landlord of the tenant's property by imposing on the landlord the obligation to compensate an outgoing tenant for his improvements. The right of the tenant to security of tenure was admitted by compelling the landlord to "compensate for disturbance" if he ejected his tenant, and by authorising the tenant to keep possession of his holding until the money was paid. In cases of dispute, the amount of compensation was to be decided by the Civil Bill Court (County Court); a scale, however, limiting to far too low a sum the maximum amount that could be fixed as compensation for disturbance, was inserted in the Act. Unfortunately the object of the Legislature in passing the Bill was foiled, for it made no provision for preventing the landlord raising the rent when improvements were made by the tenant, and so confiscation went on unchecked; if the tenant tried to avoid the penalty by giving notice to quit on the raising of the rent he received no compensation for disturbance, the compensation being only paid when he was "disturbed in his holding by the act of his landlord". The attempt to create a peasant proprietary also proved a failure, for though the Government was authorised to advance two-thirds of the purchase-money to a cultivator desiring to buy land, the legal expenses were so heavy as to prove practically prohibitory. A fairly extensive sale of Church lands, however, took place, the legal cost being far less, and between five and six thousand peasant proprietors were thus made.

The failure of this effort to settle the Irish land question, and the sufferings inflicted on the people by famine, led to continued agitation, and one of the first measures introduced by Mr. Gladstone's Government in the short session of 1880 was the Compensation for Disturbance Bill (Ireland). It was rejected by the House of Lords by a majority of 232, and the agitation in Ireland passed, as Mr. Gladstone had predicted, into a state which was practically one of civil war. In 1881 the second great Irish Land Act was passed, which laid down the important principle of a "judicial rent". It also established Land Courts, which were empowered to fix these judicial rents, and these Courts have largely reduced the rack-rents before exacted.

While these two great Irish measures are of vital importance as laying down the principle of State interference between landlord and tenant, other measures affecting the Tenure of Land were passed during this same fruitful period. The Agricultural Holdings Act of 1875 was, like the Artisans' Dwellings Act, permissive, and those whom it is most necessary to coerce thus escape from its provisions. In 1879 an attempt to abolish distraint for rent of agricultural holdings was made by Mr. Blennerhassett, but he was defeated by a majority of 110, and nothing was done for tenants until a Liberal Government was again in power. In 1880 the Ground Game Bill was passed, authorising farmers to kill ground game on their own farms, so relieving them from the obligation of feeding their landlords' animals, so far as quadrupeds were concerned. The landlords are still allowed to keep winged game at their tenants' expense, and avail themselves largely of this legalised form of theft.

The system of National Education, commenced in 1839, assumed definite shape and wide extent in 1870. In that year Mr. Forster brought in his famous Bill of Elementary Education and carried it to a successful issue. By this Act it was declared that "there shall be provided for every school district a sufficient amount of accommodation in public elementary schools (as hereinafter defined) available for all the children resident in such district for whose elementary education efficient and suitable provision is not otherwise made". Religious liberty was guarded by enacting that "it shall not be required, as a condition of any child being admitted into or continuing in the school, that he shall attend or abstain from attending any Sunday school, or any place of religious worship, or that he shall attend any religious observance or any instruction in religious subjects in the school or elsewhere": any religious instruction given at the school was to be given at the beginning or end of the schoolhours, and any parent might withdraw his child; the inspector was not to have the duty of examining in religious knowledge. Each child was to pay a weekly fee, unless excused on the ground of the parent's poverty, and if "a school board satisfy the Education Department that, on the ground of the poverty of the inhabitants of any place in this district, it is expedient for the interests of education to provide a school at which no fees shall be required from the scholars, the board may, subject to such rules and conditions as the Education Department may prescribe, provide such school, and may admit scholars to such school without requiring any fee". Expenses were to be met out of the "school fund", which consisted of moneys received as fees, provided by Parliament, raised by loan or by rate: further, one district might be directed to "contribute towards the provision or maintenance of public elementary schools in another school district or districts". School Boards, to carry out the duties imposed by the Act, were to be elected by the ratepayers by the cumulative vote, and these Boards might pass a bye-law rendering education compulsory for children between the ages of five and thirteen, any child over ten years of age being exempted from the bye-law if he was certified as having reached the standard of education fixed by the Board. Such is an outline of the famous Education Act, the first effective attempt to educate the children of the poor. The amending Act of 1873 contains nothing but matters of detail, with the exception of the proviso that if any parent was receiving out-door relief, it was to "be a condition for the continuance of such relief that elementary education in reading, writing, and arithmetic" should be given to any child between the ages of five and thirteen. In 1876 another Education Act was passed. By this it was declared that "it shall be the duty of the parent of every child to cause such child to receive efficient elementary instruction in reading, writing, and arithmetic, and if such parent fail to perform such duty, he shall be liable to such orders and penalties as are provided by this Act". The Act forbade the employment of children under ten years of age, and of children above that age if they had not reached a certain standard of education, unless such children were attending school during part of the day. Local authorities were empowered to authorise the employment of children over eight years of age, for not more than six weeks in the year, in husbandry or ingathering of crops. Provision was made for compelling the parent to send his child to school, and in case of non-compliance with the order a court of summary jurisdiction was authorised to send the child to a certified day industrial school. In such schools meals were to be provided, and were to be paid for "out of moneys provided by Parliament" and by fees paid by the parents, the latter to be excused if the parent were too poor to pay them, and to be charged on the rates. It is noteworthy that in all cases of payment of fees for parents, provided for in this and in the Act of 1870, the payment is not to be taken as making the parent a pauper; thus, in this Act of 1876 it is laid down: "The parent shall not by reason of any payment made under this section be deprived of any franchise, right, or privilege, or be subject to any disability or disqualification".

As in the former period, from 1832 to 1867, the struggle for a free press accompanied Parliamentary action in favor of education, so in the period we are now considering, another great step was taken towards freeing the press from its shackles. The combatant in this struggle was Charles Bradlaugh, and the battle was over the Act imposing sureties against blasphemy and sedition, 60 George III., cap. 9. This Act was intended to stop "pamphlets and printed papers, containing observations upon public events and occurrences, tending to excite hatred and contempt of the Government and constitution of these realms, as to law established, and also vilifying our holy religion". It applied only to publications sold at less than sixpence per copy. Mr. Bradlaugh, as editor of the *National Reformer*, a Republican and Freethought twopenny journal, declined to give sureties, on the ground that so doing would make the conduct of the paper too costly for his means. For some years the paper went on its way, all applications for the security being met with a bland refusal. At last, in 1868, the Tory Government resolved to prosecute, and the paper appeared with a line under its heading: "Published in defiance of Her Majesty's Government, and of the 60th George III., cap. 9" (*National Reformer*, May 3rd, 1868, p. 281). Mr. Bradlaugh's answer to the notice of prosecution was characteristic:

"TO HER MAJESTY'S COMMISSIONERS FOR THE DEPARTMENT OF INLAND REVENUE.

"GENTLEMEN,—You have taken the pains to officially remind me of an Act of Parliament, passed in 1819, avowedly for the suppression of cheap Democratic and Freethought literature, and you require me to comply with its provisions, such provisions being absolutely prohibitory to the further appearance of this journal. With all humility, I am obliged to bid you defiance; you may kill the *National Reformer*, but it will not commit suicide. Before you destroy my paper we shall have to fight the question, so far as my means will permit me.

"I know the battle is not on equal terms. You have the national purse, I an empty pocket; you have the trained talent of the law officers of the Crown, I my own poor wits. But it would be cowardly indeed in me to shrink in 1868 from a contest in which my gallant predecessor, Richard Carlile, fought so persistently more than a quarter of a century since."

This is not the place to record the varying events of the long struggle; it must suffice to say that Sir John Karslake failed, in consequence of the adroit legal fencing of his lay opponent, and that the Gladstone Government, coming into office, disgraced itself by taking up the prosecution in 1869. The Crown gained a verdict, which Mr. Bradlaugh upset; a *stet processus* was then entered. the Government introducing a Bill to repeal the Acts. Mr. Ayrton had previously endeavored to get rid of these oppressive laws, having described them as "laws which could never have been placed upon the statute-book except in the most evil times, when the old Tory party was engaged in desperate struggles to repress the expression of public opinion, and to maintain its hold of political power". Now his bill passed rapidly through its stages, and the freedom of the press was won as far as political discussion was concerned. From that time forward cheap newspapers could circulate, criticising all flaws, advocating all reforms, without fear of having to pay for their boldness by the forfeiture of their recognisances, and that freedom they owe to that small but gallant party which since the time of Thomas Paine has fought and suffered for the liberty of all.

III.—Results of the Reform Bill of 1884.

In the previous pages I have tried to trace the results of Reform as seen exemplified in our past. In the following ones I propose to outline results which are yet in the future, but which lie in the direct line of evolution, and are but an expansion and a development of principles already accepted by the Legislature. What legislative action is likely to be taken by the Reformed Parliament with respect to the conditions of Labor, Religious Liberty and Equality, the Tenure of Land, the Education of the People? As in the past, so in the future, the new Parliament will be full of reforming energy; again we stand on the threshold of great changes, changes to which some look with fear and some with hope.

We have already seen that the principle of legislative interference between employers and employed has been largely acted on by Parliament since 1832. There is no reason to suppose that the new Parliament will be more careless of the interests of the workers than its predecessors have been; indeed, elected as it will be, by a larger number of handworkers than have ever before taken part in the choice of representatives of the Commons, it will probably be more inclined to legislate in the interests of Labor than any Parliament we have yet seen.

The hours of labor have been shortened at successive intervals since 1801, and it is not unreasonable to suppose that a further shortening of these hours will soon be made. The ordinary London operative now works for a ten hours' day, from 6 a.m. to 5 p.m. with an hour's interval for dinner. Mr. Howell says on this: "If we take the metropolis we shall find that a building operative has to be at his work at six o'clock in the morning, and he now leaves at five o'clock at night. But he has often to walk four or five miles to his work, so that he has to leave home at five and cannot reach home again until six, making a total of thirteen hours. . . . An hour's walk is often very exhilarating to a business man, shut up in an office all day, but to a mason, carpenter, bricklayer, or plasterer, who has frequently to plod through the rain or drifting snow, it is painfully exhausting, especially when it has to be done before six o'clock in the morning."[1]

There can be no doubt in the minds of reasonable people that a ten hours' day is too long. But if that be so, what shall we say to the hours of labor of shopmen and shopwomen, who in most large shops in London begin at 8 a.m. or 9 a.m. and continue at work until 7 p.m. or 8 p.m.? In the smaller shops things are still worse, and, going through a poor neighborhood, we see provision shops open until 10 p.m. or even 11 p.m. served by exhausted men and women, whose pale cheeks and languid movements tell of the strain which is destroying their vitality. The new Parliament should pass an Eight Hours Bill, making the legal day a day of eight hours only, and giving one half-holiday in the week, so that the weekly hours of labor shall not exceed forty-four. In time to come I trust that the hours of labor will be yet further shortened, but the

---

[1] "The Conflicts of Capital and Labor." By G. Howell. Pp. 295, 296.

passage of an Eight Hours Bill would mark a good step forward. Looking at the question from a rational point of view, it is surely clear that a human being should not be required to give more than eight hours out of the twenty-four—one third of his time—for absolute bread-winning. Another seven or eight hours must be given to sleep, leaving eight for meals, exercise, recreation, and study. The last eight are short enough for their varied uses, and I look forward to a time when the first section shall be shortened and the third lengthened; but if every worker had even eight hours of freedom in the day, his life would be a far more human and far more beautiful thing than it is at the present time.

The establishment of an eight hours' day would also help to distribute toil a little more evenly than it is distributed now; the same amount of work will have to be performed, and if each pair of hands only does $\frac{4}{5}$ of the work it now does, additional pairs of hands must execute the remainder. At present some are being worn out with excessive labor, while others are clamoring for employment; shorter hours for the present workers mean work for the now idle hands.

Legislation on the sanitary—or rather insanitary—conditions of various trades is urgently required. I need only mention the whitelead makers, the Sheffield grinders, the miners in dangerous workings, to remind my readers of well-known scandals. Some would leave all remedial measures to voluntary effort and to the influence of "humanity". But humanity looks on them indifferently to-day: it shops at all hours, careless of the suffering inflicted: it says "How sad!" when it reads of special distress, and goes on with its dinner: it contemplates the conditions under which they live who feed and clothe and serve it, and murmurs platitudes about "differences of ranks", and happiness being "pretty evenly distributed, after all": and so it will remain until the strong arm of the law shall compel it to do justice, and shall force it to yield as obedience what it will never yield to prayer.

We may reasonably hope that Religious Liberty and Equality will be rendered complete by the new Parliament. The liberty to make an affirmation in all cases in which an oath is now required will, I trust, be granted by the present Legislature; if not, the passage of an Affirmation

Bill will be one of the first duties of the Reformed Parliament. An amending Burials Bill, giving to unbelievers the right to an "orderly service" at the graveside (see p. 18), will probably pass without much difficulty. Nor is there much likelihood of serious opposition to a Bill for repealing "all the statutes inflicting penalties for opinion, or placing hindrances in the way of lectures and discussions", and for annulling "the present penal and disabling effect of the common law".[1] The general confession by hostile Christians that the latest prosecutions for blasphemy have only injured their religion and strengthened Freethought, shows that the rusty sword of persecution is not likely to be often used by them in the future, and it is noticeable that Radical candidates for the next Parliament are very generally pledging themselves to a repeal of the obnoxious statutes.

There remains the greatest of all the religious changes—the disestablishment and disendowment of the English, Welsh, and Scotch Churches: the public national confession that henceforward the State will concern itself only with the conduct and no longer with the speculations of its citizens. The disestablishment of the Churches will be easily enough effected; the English and Welsh bishops will disappear from the House of Lords as quietly as did their Irish brethren, to the advantage of that House, by the removal of a special obstructiveness, and, let us hope, to the advantage of those dioceses to which their attention will thenceforth be more completely confined. The disendowment clauses of the Bill will present far more difficulty, not only from the vast wealth with which they will deal, but also from the complexity of the interests concerned. The cry of "Sacrilege" and of "Robbery" is sure to be raised when Parliament lays its hands on "Church property". Those who use such epithets will have to be reminded that an enormous part of the Church's wealth is drawn from lands given to the Roman Catholic Church by pious Papists, and that if it be theft for the State to divert to new ends property given to a corporation within its limits, then the first theft was made when Henry VIII. by Act of Parliament severed the Church in England from

---

[1] "The Laws relating to Blasphemy and Heresy." By Charles Bradlaugh. P. 31.

the Papal obedience, and it does not lie with the receiver of stolen goods to complain of robbery when the goods are again removed. Every one knows that many fellowships of the Universities of Oxford and Cambridge were charged with the payment of masses for the souls of the defunct donors; Protestants who regard masses for the dead as "dangerous deceits" have gaily pocketed the Papists' money, and have left their souls unprayed and unpaid for. The Church as by law established has been quite content to fatten on the spoils of its Roman predecessor, and it is with but a bad grace that it commences to pose as the injured innocent, when a second transfer of the cash is proposed. The ground which we should take in dealing with Church funds is a simple one; the State cannot allow the hands of long-mouldered corpses to determine the disposition of wealth now in its midst, and is itself the supreme arbiter in dispensing huge accumulations made by the generations of its dead. Funds which are annually voted to the Church can be stopped by omission of the votes; the rest must be dealt with by the Bill. It is earnestly to be hoped that the State will retain in its own hands all the glebe lands. Their rental will then form a source of national income and will go to lighten the general burden of taxation. The rental of the ecclesiastical buildings to bodies desiring to use them for religious worship, lectures, etc., will form another large item on the credit side of the national balance-sheet. Some provision out of these funds will have to be made for the aged beneficed clergy, as it would be cruel to turn them out helpless into the world. The clergy of the future will have to be supported by their own congregations, as Dissenting ministers are supported now, and "Church people" will no longer be religious paupers, with their souls fed and clothed at the expense of their neighbors.

Changes in the Tenure of Land, vaster than any hitherto attempted, will probably be made by the Reformed Parliament. The huge masses of agricultural laborers now dowered with the vote have been wearing the agricultural shoe long enough to know where it pinches, and they are likely to prove energetic shoemakers. The changes to be made will be radical changes, involving the substitution of a rational system of land-holding for the quasi-feudal one now existing. The new system will be based on the recognition of the principle that land, being the sole fundamental means of existence for all, cannot expediently be regarded as the private property of individuals. Since men can only live by virtue of what they obtain from land, so long as land belongs to a set of individuals in a nation the remainder of the nation must work for these at whatever wages they will give, and freedom of contract between those who hold the means of existence and those who need them becomes a meaningless phrase. Hence, unearned accumulations of wealth for the privileged class, and continual struggle for existence for the unprivileged, with an ever-widening gulf between the unjustly rich and unjustly poor. The substitution of the new system for the old implies too vast a change to be wrought at once; but it is essential that every alteration made in the present tenure of land shall be an alteration tending towards the goal of nationalisation, and not a mere tinkering of abuses on the present basis. The more drastic of the proposals put forward by the Land Law Reform League should be transformed into law by the new Parliament. (I omit the suggested reforms on which all Liberals are agreed, such as cheap transfer, security for improvements, etc.) Thus: cultivable land kept uncultivated and not used for public purposes should be forfeit to the State, "with payment to the dispossessed landowner of say twenty years' purchase at the average annual value of the land for the seven years prior to the" dispossession. "Annual value" is to be understood as meaning any amount really obtained from actual produce: in many shameful cases this is only a few head of game. "Payment to be made by bonds of the State, bearing the same interest as the consolidated debt." "*The land to be State property*, and to be let to actual tenant cultivators. . . . The amount paid as rent to the State to be applied to the payment of the interest [on the bonds], and to form a sinking fund for the liquidation of the principal." The words I have italicised are of vital importance; this forfeited land is not to be sold; it is to be let by the State. Thus the State will become a landholder on a large scale, and a huge step towards nationalisation will be made. The glebe lands above spoken of will add another great slice to the national estate, and no acre of land acquired by the State must ever again be sold to an individual. The breaking up of large estates and the further acquisition of land by the State will be brought about by the imposition of a graduated land tax, "say, the normal tax on the first 5,000 acres, a double tax on the second 5,000 acres, again doubled on the next 10,000 acres," and so on. As the amount thus imposed as tax would soon exceed the value of the land, unduly large estates would be made untenable, and the owners would be forced to sell. "Re-valuation of lands for the more equitable imposition of the land tax" is another matter of pressing importance, the nominal tax of 4s. in the £ being in many cases now a real tax of ¾d., 1d., or 1½d. If the land-tax were levied on the present value of land, instead of on the value it had nearly 200 years ago, it would amount to about £50,000,000 a year, and this fourth part of the income from land would go into the Exchequer of the State, instead of into the ever-gaping pockets of the privileged class.

Before very long, also, Parliament must take into consideration cases like those of the Dukes of Portland, Bedford, and Westminster, whose predecessors let out land on building leases, and who come into possession, as the leases fall in, of houses to the building of which they have not contributed a penny. This shameful confiscation of other people's property should be stopped and that speedily, or else we may hereafter be called on to compensate these all-swallowers for depriving them of property to which they have not the smallest title, and which they should not be allowed to acquire.

The Education of the young will, I hope, receive at the hands of the Reformed Parliaments wide extension and development. The State schools will probably become entirely secular, religious education being left to the various religious sects and to teachers selected by the parents. Compulsion will be enacted by the law of the land, instead of by bye-laws as at present. School fees paid by the parent, already avoidable by the very poor, will be entirely abolished, and the whole cost of education will be charged on the rates, instead of the greater part only, as at present. The abolition of these will relieve the teachers from much heavy clerical work, now imposed on them; will do away with all the machinery for enquiry which now exists to deal with cases in which the remission of fees is asked; and will reduce to a minimum the prosecutions for non-attendance, and the cost of the army of officials now needed to enforce it. Thus will the work of 1870 and 1876 be completed, and we shall have a system of National Education, secular, compulsory, and rate-supported.

What shall be included in this education is a question too wide for discussion at the close of this paper. I look forward to a time when every child shall receive in the national schools the elements of a literary, scientific, artistic, and technical education; when neither boy nor girl shall leave the school ignorant of the glories of our literature, of the wonders of science, of the delight in beauty, of some definite means of bread-winning. Be it tailoring, or dress-making, or cookery, or carpentering, or any one of the many trades needed in a civilised society, every pair of hands should be able to do at least some one thing well, by which a living may be honestly earned. The maturity that follows a youth spent in such training will be useful to the State, and enjoyable to the individual; and such a maturity it should be the object of educational laws to make possible for every citizen.

The lines here sketched are not likely to be followed out in any one Parliament, however great the impulse for improvement, but it is along these lines that the reforming energy will travel, if the study of the past shed any light upon the future of Reform.

THE

EVOLUTION OF SOCIETY.

BY

ANNIE BESANT.

[Reprinted from *Our Corner.*]

LONDON:
FREETHOUGHT PUBLISHING COMPANY,
63, FLEET STREET, E.C.
1886.

PRICE THREEPENCE.

THE EVOLUTION OF SOCIETY.

THE recognition of Evolution in the physical world, of gradual progress from the simple to the complex, of reiterated integration as the steps of that progress, has led to the application of the same unifying principle to the psychical world, and to the suggestion of its application to the sociological. As the lowest forms of life consist of simple independent cells, as these cells become grouped, differentiated, integrated into tissues, as these tissues become more complex in arrangement, more co-ordinated, in the highest organisms, so, it is argued, do the individual human units become grouped into families and tribes, integrated into a social organism, of which the multiplicity of the composing elements is the measure of its adaptability, the unity and the correlation thereof the measure of its strength. If Society be thus regarded as an organism instead of as a bag of marbles, if it be conceded that the health of the whole depends upon the healthy functioning of every part, in correlation not in independence, then all that tends towards integration will be recognised as of life, all that tends towards disintegration as of death. Judging the future by the past we shall be prepared to look forward to the realisation of a fuller social unity than has yet been reached, and to recognise that by an inexorable necessity Society must either integrate yet further, or must begin a movement which will result in its resolution into its elements. The further integration may be regarded as an ideal to be embraced, or as a doom to be striven against, as a brotherhood to be rejoiced in or as a slavery to be abhorred;

but the believer in Evolution must acknowledge that if Society is to endure, this further integration is inevitable.

The object of this and of the following papers is to roughly outline this Evolution of Society, and to consider the type towards which it is working; and they will deal with: I. The Barbaric Period and its Survivals; II. The Industrial Period and its products; III. The Conflict between Social and Anti-Social Tendencies; IV. The Reconcilement of Diverging Interests.

I.—The Barbaric Period and its Survivals.

Association for the common weal is, as is well known, by no means confined to man. Many herbivorous animals live in herds, and in the pastures the females and the young graze in the centre, while the males form a protective ring, and sentinels, carefully posted, give warning cries of alarm if danger approaches. Wolves hunt in packs, and together pull down prey with which singly they could not cope. Bees and ants live in thickly populated communities, with their builders, food-gatherers, nurses, and in many cases soldiers, all working for the Society as a whole. Man's nearest congeners, the apes, are social animals and differ little in their qualities and morality from the lowest savages. And in all these one phænomenon is noteworthy: the submission of the individual to restraints for the general good. When a tribe of monkeys goes out on a predatory expedition—as to rob an orchard—the young ones are slapped if they are not silent and obedient. When a goat is discharging a sentinel's duty, he may not feed at ease on the tempting grass on which his comrades are luxuriating, confident in his vigilant loyalty. The working-bee must not keep the honey it gathers, but must carry it home for storing. Each member of the community yields up something of individual freedom, receiving in exchange the benefits of association, and it is among those who—like the bees and ants—have carried very far the subordination of the unit to the social organism that the most successful communities are found.

In the Barbaric Period of human society the virtues evolved are much the same as those which characterise the brute communities—courage, discipline of a rudimentary kind, loyalty to the head of the tribe. These are evolved because they are necessary to the success of the tribe, and those who are weak in them perish in the struggle for existence. They are evolved by the pressure of necessity, by the exigencies of the common life. As disputes can only be settled by war, the military chief is indispensable, and the strong and cunning man is made the head of the community. As social conditions become a little more settled, and the conventions which grew up from necessity become gradually crystallised into law, the hereditary principle creeps in, and the most capable adult member of a family —now recognised as royal—is selected to fill the throne; as law increases yet more in authority, the personal capacity of the sovereign becames a matter of less vital necessity, and the eldest son succeeds to his father's crown, whether he is major or minor; at last the time is reached, as with ourselves, in which a monarch is simply a survival, interesting—as are all rudimentary organs, because marks of an ancestral condition—but perfectly useless: a mere excrescence like the dew-claw of a St. Bernard dog. Essentially barbaric, it is an anachronism in a civilised society, and only endures by virtue of its inoffensiveness and of the public inertia.

Still keeping within the Barbaric Period, but passing out of the stage in which every man was a warrior, we come to the time in which Society was constituted of two classes: the fighting class, which consisted of king and nobles; the working class, which consisted of those who toiled on the land and of all engaged in commerce of any kind, whether by producing goods for sale or by selling them when produced. The fighting class had then its real utility; if the king and the nobles claimed the privilege of governing, they discharged the duty of protecting, and while they tyrannised and robbed at home to a considerable extent, they defended against foreign oppression the realm to which they belonged. Fighting animals they were, like the big-jawed soldiers of the Termites, but they were necessary while the nations had not emerged from barbarism. But these were not in the line of evolution; the evolving life of the nation was apart from them; they were the wall that protected, that encircled the life that was developing, and their descendants are but the crumbling ruins which mark where once the bastions and the ramparts frowned.

The life of the nation was in its workers, among whom the agriculturists claim our first attention. The villeins who tilled the soil under the feudal system were, in a very real sense, the chattels of their lord. They were bound to the soil, might be recovered by a legal suit if they left their lord's estate, were liable to seizure of all their property by their lord at his mere will, might be imprisoned or assaulted by him, and in many cases the lord held over them a power of life and death. These feudal privileges of the lord gradually disappeared in England during the Middle Ages; many villeins fled their native soil, hired themselves out in other parts of the country, and were never recovered by their lords; residence for a year and a day in a walled town made a villein free: relaxations of servitude made by an indulgent lord became customary: villeins became transformed into copyholders in many cases, and in one way or another the peasantry emerged from nominal slavery.

In trying to realise the lot of the villein and to compare it with that of his modern descendant, the agricultural laborer, it is not sufficient to study only the conditions of his servitude, the extreme roughness and poorness of his house, his ignorance, the frequent scarcity and general coarseness of his food. It must be remembered that if his lord was his owner he was also his protector, and that the landowner's feeling of duty to his tenants and the tenants' feeling of dependence and claim for assistance on the landowner which still exist in some old-world parts of England, are survivals of the old feudal tie which implied subjection without consciousness of degradation. Further, while the hut of the villein was of the poorest kind, the castle of the lord by no means realised our modern idea of a comfortable house: the villein had straw on his floor, but the lord had only rushes; and the general roughness of the time effected all alike. If the villein was ignorant, so was the lord, and if the lord tilted gaily with the lance, the villein broke heads as gaily with his staff. If the villein was sometimes sorely put to it to find bread, at other times he revelled in rough abundance, and the doles at the monastery gates often eked out his scanty supply when Nature was unkind. Speaking broadly, there was far less difference then in fashion of living between lord and villein than now between lord and laborer: less difference of taste, of amusements, of education, and therefore more comradeship: the baron's retainers then dined at the table of the lord without shocking any fastidious taste, while my lord marquis now would find his dinner much interfered with if his servants sat at it as of old. And since happiness is very much a matter of comparison, it may be doubted whether the villein was not happier than the agricultural laborer is now, and whether the lop-sided progress of Society, which has given so little to the toiler in comparison with what it has given to the idler, has been much of a blessing to the laboring agricultural class.

The growth of industries other than agricultural marked with unmistakable distinctness the evolution of society from barbarism. Handworkers in these tended to produce in groups, and soon associated themselves in towns, partly for convenience in production and distribution, partly for self-defence; divorced from the land, they were naturally less directly dependent on the landowners than were the agriculturists, and as the king's wish to plunder them was checked by the nobles, and the nobles' wish to plunder by the king, they gradually secured charters which protected them from both, and waxed free and prosperous. Each craft had its guild, and the apprentice entering to learn his trade worked his way step by step up to the position of a master craftsman. There were then no large aggregations of workers, as in our modern factories, but the lad placed in a workshop was one of a small group, and was trained as a member of a family rather than as a "hand". Entrance into the workshop of a famous master was eagerly sought for, and in consequence of the slight division of labor there was a pride in capable workmanship which is now almost impossible. Individual ability, under this system, was at once apparent and had scope for development, so that art and industry were more closely united than they have ever been since. The artist was largely a handicraftsman in the industrial sense, and the handicraftsman was largely an artist; and side by side with this mental development existed physical vigor, in consequence of the small size of the towns and the accessibility of the open country. In industrial pursuits, as in those of the countryside, the great division between classes which is now so grievous did not exist; the "master" worked with his men, eat with them, lived with them, and the "industrious apprentice" who "married his master's daughter" was not a poetic fiction, but an inspiring and realisable ideal. Certainly the amount of products turned out could not rival the vast quantities now produced, but the lives of the producers were healthier and more human than those of too many of the handicraftsmen of to-day.

Among the survivals from the Barbaric Period present in modern society, the monarch has already been mentioned. Perhaps no form of monarchy exposes its anachronistic character more completely than the "limited monarchy" of modern England. There is an exquisite absurdity in the man who *can* being changed into the man who can *not*.[1] The hereditary aristocracy is another survival from barbarism, and is a curious travesty of the scientific truth as to race. The analogy of a high-bred horse and a high-bred man is misleading, for the human breeding is a matter of name, not of qualities. There can be no doubt that a human aristocracy might be bred, by matching men and women who showed in marked degree the qualities which might be selected as admirable, but the aristocracy which proceeds from male idlers, profligate in their undisciplined youth and luxurious in their pampered maturity, matched with female idlers, whose uselessness, vanity, and extravagance are their chief recommendations, is not one which should bear rule in a strong and intellectual nation. To the barbaric Past it belongs, not to the semi-civilised Present, and the lease of its power will be determined when the workers realise the power which has now passed into their hands.

II.—The Industrial Period and its Products.

The Industrial Period may fairly be taken as beginning for all practical purposes with the invention of the Spinning Jenny by Hargreaves, a weaver, in 1764; of the Spinning Machine by Arkwright, a barber, in 1768; of the Mule, by Crompton, a weaver, 1776. If to these we add the virtual invention of the Steam Engine by Watt in 1765, we have within these twelve years, from 1764 to 1776, the vastest revolution in industry the world has known, the birth of a new Period in the Evolution of Society. As

---

[1] King, German *König*, has the same root as *Können*, to be able.

Green points out in his "History of the English People", the "handloom used in the Manchester cotton trade had until that time retained the primitive shape which is still found in the handlooms of India" (p. 768), and the conditions of labor were feudal, patriarchic, domestic, not industrial, in the modern sense of the word. The introduction of machinery (other than the simple kinds used in earlier times) revolutionised social life as well as industry, and the vast increase of man's power over nature not only affected the production of manufactured goods, but affected also the condition of the worker, the climate and aspect of the country, as also, with the most far-reaching results, the framework and tendencies of society. These all are the products of the Industrial Period, and these all must be taken into consideration if we would estimate fairly and fully the net result of good or of evil which remains.

It is obvious that the great value of machinery lies in the fact that it produces much with little labor; in the words of a Report: "One man in a cotton-mill superintends as much work as could have been done by two hundred, seventy years ago." The result of this should have been widespread comfort, general sufficiency of the necessaries of life, a great diminution of the hours of labor: the result of it has been the accumulation of vast fortunes by a comparatively few, the deadening and the brutalising of crowds of the handworkers. Whether we regard the immediate or the general results, we shall find them very different from the rosy hopes of those who gave to the world the outcome of their inventive genius.

The immediate result of the introduction of machinery was, as everyone knows, terrible suffering among handicraftsmen. Let us hear Green, an impartial witness. "Manufactures profited by the great discoveries of Watt and Arkwright; and the consumption of raw cotton in the mills of Lancashire rose during the same period from fifty to a hundred millions of pounds. The vast accumulation of capital, as well as the constant recurrence of bad seasons at this time, told upon the land, and forced agriculture into a feverish and unhealthy prosperity. Wheat rose to famine prices, and the value of land rose in proportion with the price of wheat. Inclosures went on with prodigious rapidity; the income of every landowner was doubled, while the farmers were able to introduce improvements into the processes of agriculture which changed the whole face of the country. But if the increase of wealth was enormous, its distribution was partial. During the fifteen years which preceded Waterloo, the number of the population rose from ten to thirteen millions, and this rapid increase kept down the rate of wages, which would naturally have advanced in a corresponding degree with the increase of the national wealth. Even manufactures, though destined in the long run to benefit the laboring classes, seemed at first rather to depress them. One of the earliest results of the introduction of machinery was the ruin of a number of small trades which were carried on at home, and the pauperisation of families who relied on them for support. In the winter of 1811 the terrible pressure of this transition from handicraft to machinery was seen in the Luddite, or machine-breaking, riots which broke out over the northern and midland counties, and which were only suppressed by military force. While labor was thus thrown out of its older grooves, and the rate of wages kept down at an artificially low figure by the rapid increase of population, the rise in the price of wheat, which brought wealth to the landowner and the farmer, brought famine and death to the poor, for England was cut off by the war from the vast cornfields of the Continent or of America, which nowadays redress from their abundance the results of a bad harvest. Scarcity was followed by a terrible pauperisation of the laboring classes. The amount of the poor-rate rose fifty per cent., and with the increase of poverty followed its inevitable result, the increase of crime" ("Hist. of the English People", pp. 805, 806).

It is noteworthy that where handworkers are concerned, no claim for compensation is ever put forward when they are deprived of their means of livelihood. If it is proposed to nationalise the land, it is at once alleged that the present owners must be bought out, on the ground that it would be unjust to deprive them of their incomes from land and to reduce them to poverty for the benefit of the community. But no one is so scrupulous, or so tender-hearted, when only laborers are ruined; no one ever proposed to compensate the handicraftsmen who were robbed of their means of existence by the introduction of machinery. Great stress is laid on the general benefit of the community, for which it appears it is right to sacrifice the worker, but wrong to sacrifice the idler. And further, if a starving laborer fall back on the poor-rate he is at once "pauperised", and everyone knows it is a disgrace to be a pauper—on the parish: but if a Duke of Marlborough, with huge estates, pockets a sum of £107,000 out of the taxes he is not "pauperised", and everyone knows it is no disgrace to be a pauper—on the nation.

The general result of the introduction of machinery has clearly been a great increase of comfort and wealth to the upper and middle classes, and to the upper stratum of the artisans; but great masses of the people are worse off absolutely, as well as relatively, in consequence of its introduction. They are more crowded together, the air they breathe is fouler, the food they eat is more unwholesome, the trades they live by are more ruinous to health, than they were in the time when towns were smaller, the open country more accessible, the air unpoisoned by factory chimneys and chemical works; the times when "master and man" slept in the same house, dined at the same table, worked in the same room.

Machinery has enormously increased the amount of goods produced, but it has not lightened the toil of the workers; it has sent down prices, but the laborer must work as long to gain his bare subsistence. The introduction of sewing-machines may serve as a typical instance. It was said that they would lighten the toil of the needlewoman, and enable her to earn a livelihood more easily. Nothing of the sort has happened; the needlewoman works for quite as many hours, and earns quite as meagre a subsistence; she makes three or four coats where before she made one, but her wages are not trebled or quadrupled; the profits of her employer are increased, and coats are sold at a lower price. The real value of machinery, again, may be seen when a sewing machine is introduced into a house where the needlework is done at home; there the toil *is* lightened; the necessary work is done in a fifth part of the time, and the workers have leisure instead of long hours of labor. The inference is irresistible; machinery is of enormous value in lessening human toil when it is owned by those who produce, and who produce for use, not for profit; it is not of value to those who work it for wages, for the wages depend, not on the worth of the goods produced, but on the competition in the labor-market and the cost of subsistence.

In dealing with the products of the Industrial Period, the human products are of the most extreme importance. How have the conditions of labor, the environment, and therefore the life of the laborer, been affected by the introduction of machinery? I say, without fear of contradiction, that the environment of the manufacturing laborers has altered for the worse, and that the result of that worsening may be seen in the physical deterioration of the great masses of the workers in factory towns. Compare the tall, upright, brown laborer of Lincolnshire with the short, bowed, pallid knife-grinder of Sheffield; compare the robust, stalwart Northumberland miner with the slender, pasty-cheeked lads who come trooping out of a Manchester cotton-mill; and you will soon see the physical difference caused by difference of labor-conditions. Sheffield workers die young, their lungs choked with the metal dust they inhale; cotton-factory "hands" die of the fibre-laden air they breathe. I grant that Sheffield goods are cheap, if by cheapness is meant that fewer coins are paid for them than would have been required ere they were made by machinery; but to me those things are not cheap which are rendered less in money-cost by destruction of human life. Hood once wrote of cheap shirts:

> "O men with sisters dear,
> O men with mothers and wives,
> It is not linen you're wearing out,
> But human creatures' lives!"

And to me there is many a "cheap" article which is dear by the price that has been paid for its cheapness, price of human health, price of human happiness, price of human life, making it costly beyond all reckoning, for it incarnates the misery of the poor.

I grant readily that things were worse before the Factory Acts were passed; but this truth only makes me desire their extension, and also a far greater insistence on sanitation than at present prevails. It is necessary that a large number of workers should co-operate in production by machinery; it is not necessary that they should be poisoned or wearied out with toil. The working-day should be short, because mechanical toil tends to stupefy; and every factory should have a recreation-ground, prettily laid out, with facilities for games, to which the workers might resort for the intervals between the hours of labor. Thorough ventilation should ensure the wholesomeness of the air within the factory, a task which would be greatly facilitated by each factory standing alone and being tree-surrounded.

The law should also promptly concern itself with the scandalous pollution of the atmosphere and of rivers by the smoke and refuse of factories. There is no reason why every factory should not consume its own smoke, and the law already existing on this matter should be sternly enforced, by imprisonment, not by fine. A man who poisons one person is punished; a man who poisons a whole neighborhood goes free. The thick cloud of black smoke hanging over a town like Sheffield or Manchester is a sickening sight; it blights the trees, destroys the flowers, soils every house, dirties every article of clothing. Who that has lived in Manchester can forget "Manchester blacks"? It is pitiable to go through the country and see exquisite landscapes destroyed by smoke and refuse; huge chimneys belching out black torrents; streams that should be dancing in the sunlight gleaming with phosphorescent scum, and rolling along thick and black with filth. What sort of England is the Industrial Period going to leave to its successors?

If there be any truth in the scientific doctrine that the environment modifies the organism, what can be the tendency of the modifications wrought by such an environment as the Black Country? What is there of refining, of elevating, of humanising influence in those endless piles of cinders, that ruined vegetation, that pall of smoke, lighted at night by the lurid glare of the furnaces? What kind of race will that be whose mothers work in the chain-fields till the children come to the birth, and who return thither sometimes on the very day on which they have given new lives to the world?

Many people, true products of the Industrial Period, are indifferent to natural beauty, and only see in a waterfall a source of power, in a woody glen a waste of productive soil. But if, again, the environment modifies the organism, beauty is useful in the highest degree. A high human type cannot be bred in a back slum, trained amid filth and ugliness and clangor, sent to labor ere maturity; it must be bred in pure air, trained amidst sights and sounds that are harmonious and beautiful, educated until mature; then let it turn to labor, and give back to the community the wealth of love and comfort which shielded its earlier years. On the faces of the lads and lasses who come tumbling out of factories and great warehouses at the close of every day, filling the streets with tumult and rough horseplay, is set the seal of the sordid conditions under which they live. The lack of beauty around them has made them unbeautiful, and their strident voices are fitted to pierce the din amid which they live.

In truth, in its effect on Society, the wealthy manufacturing class is far worse than the feudal nobility it is gradually pushing aside. The feudal lords lived among their tenantry, and there were ties of human sympathy between them which do not exist between the manufacturer and those whom he significantly calls his "hands". The manufacturers live away from the place in which their wealth is made, dwelling luxuriously in beautiful suburbs, and leaving the "hands" to stew in closely-packed dwellings under the shadow of the huge and unsightly factories. The division of classes becomes more and more marked; between the rich and the poor yawns an ever-widening gulf.

The tendency of Industrialism to produce castes should not be overlooked. Practical men have noted that when people have for generations lived by weaving, their children learn weaving far more easily than children who come from a mining district. If a trade becomes hereditary, the aptitude for the trade becomes marked in members of the family. And this is not well. It is a tendency to produce fixed castes of workers, instead of fully-developed various human beings. It means, if present forces go on working unrestrained, the dividing of society into castes, the formation of rigid lines of demarcation, the petrifaction which has befallen some older civilisations.

Over against those who laud the present state of Society with its unjustly rich and unjustly poor, with its palaces and its slums, its millionaires and its paupers, be it ours to proclaim that there is a higher ideal in life than that of being first in the race for wealth, most successful in the scramble for gold. Be it ours to declare steadfastly that health, comfort, leisure, culture, plenty for every individual, are far more desirable than breathless struggle for existence, furious trampling down of the weak by the strong, huge fortunes accumulated out of the toil of others, to be handed down to those who have done nothing to earn them. Be it ours to maintain that the greatness of a nation depends not on the number of its great proprietors, on the wealth of its great capitalists, on the splendor of its great nobles; but on the absence of poverty among its people, on the education of its masses, on the universality of enjoyment in life.

III.—The Conflict between Social and Anti-Social Tendencies.

The conflict between social and anti-social tendencies has existed as long as Society itself. It is the contest between the integrating and disintegrating forces, between the brute survival and the human evolution. The individual struggle for existence which had gone on through countless centuries over the whole world had become to some extent modified among the social animals, and savage man, as the highest of these, had also modified it within the limits of each community. As Society progressed slowly in civilisation, the contest went on between the surviving brutal, or savage, desire for personal accumulation and personal aggrandisement without regard for others, and the social desire for general prosperity and happiness with the readiness to subordinate the individual to the general good. It is the still-enduring conflict between these tendencies which now claims our attention. The openings for personal accumulation offered during the Industrial Period gave a great impetus to the anti-social tendencies; the codification of the laws of wealth-getting in Political Economy was seized upon for defence, as though Political Economy offered any law for the general guidance of human conduct, or held up any object as the aim of human life. In their eagerness to represent as right and useful their own greed of gain, members of the *laissez-faire* school sheltered themselves under philosophic names, and used Political Economy as though instead of laying down the conditions of wealth-getting, it had declared it to be the one duty of human beings to get wealth.

The anti-social tendencies seized on three sources of

wealth as especially promising: mines, factories, landed estates. So ruinous in each department proved their unrestricted play, that in each case law had to be called in to check their operation.

MINES.—In these the anti-social tendency of unrestricted accumulation, by competition with others, led to the employment of women and children in labor for which they were unfitted, at wages lower than those obtained by men. Women worked half-naked, with band round forehead dragging laden trucks up steep inclines. Children were born in the darkness, and grew up underground, never seeing the brightness of the sun. The most frightful demoralisation existed, and infants, sleeping at their trapdoors, were crushed beneath the hurrying truck. Manly decency, womanly modesty, childly weakness, all went down before the Juggernaut car of unrestricted competition, until the social tendency, in the guise of law, stepped in to curb the brutality of anti-social greed.

FACTORIES. — Here, again, the labor of women and children has been utilised in antagonism to the better-paid labor of men. And both women and children were scandalously overworked until law intervened to protect them. In *Our Corner* for March, 1885 (vol. v., pp. 158, 159), I gave some details of the labor imposed on children before the legislature interposed, and when we find such Acts as the Factory and Workshops Acts attacked by those who pretend to defend Liberty (see report of the 3rd annual meeting of the Liberty and Property Defence League, p. 10), we know that the liberty they defend is the liberty to plunder others unchecked, the liberty which the burglar might claim in annexing his neighbors' goods. At the present time the chain-works in Warwickshire and Worcestershire show us examples of overmuch liberty in dealing with other people's lives. Women there work semi-nude, dragging heavy chains. A young girl will be absent from her work one day, and reappearing on the morrow will excuse her languid work to the inspector on the ground: "I had a baby yesterday". Child-bearing girls, to the anti-social school, are only "hands" worth so much less in the labor market. These facts have to be faced. No vague talk of "general improvement" will avail us here. These people are suffering while we are discussing, and dilettante sympathy is of small use.

LANDED ESTATES. Here, again, the anti-social tendencies have had full swing. Taxation, levied on land as the rent to the State for the privilege of holding it, has been shifted off the land on to the people, and the land has been claimed as private property instead of as public trust. Improvements made by the tenant have been confiscated, and then the improved condition of the land has been utilised as a reason for raising the rent of the tenant who improved it. Rents have been raised to an extent the tenant could not meet, until he has become hopelessly indebted to his landlord, and so bound to him, hand and foot. Game has been preserved until the crops of farmers have been ruined by it, and until wild animals luxuriated while human beings starved. When the anti-social tendency has had full play and when it has spread abroad sufficient misery for purblind eyes to recognise, then the social tendency has asserted itself, and has established Land Courts in Ireland to fix fair rents; has secured to the tenant the results of his own labor; has permitted the farmer to kill the ground game preying on his crops.

In towns the landlord has been even a greater curse than he has been in the country. Undrained, filthy, rotten hovels have been rented by him to the poor. The slums of all great cities testify to the results of the anti-social tendency, and warn us that the deepest and widest degradation will never touch men's hearts sufficiently to overbear the desire for personal gain.

Law, and law alone, can curb these anti-social tendencies. Granted that a time will come when men shall be too noble to profit by the misery of their fellows, that time is not yet. The anti-social tendencies ruin and degrade, and the few who recognise the evil while not personally experiencing it, aided by the many who suffer from it without fully understanding it, must carry legislation which shall fetter the savage inclination to prey on human beings.

So far we have considered the play of anti-social tendencies in modern society. Let us turn now to the social tendencies, to those which make for integration.

The first of these which we will note is the tendency to co-operation. Handicapped as it is by being compelled to make its way in a society based on competition, co-operation has yet done much to better the lot of the poor. How much it might do if everywhere it replaced competition, may be guessed at from what it has done despite the evil atmosphere which has surrounded it. Anyone who goes over the stores of the Rochdale Pioneers, who sees the great library it has gathered there, who knows the educational agencies centred there, must recognise the enormous good done by even partial co-operation under uncongenial circumstances. That productive co-operation has not succeeded as well as distributive is due partly to the fact that the co-operative workers have sought too eagerly and paid too highly for "influential names" to "float" their companies; and partly to the fact that production, under the present system, needs a larger capital to withstand trade crises than workers are able to command. Many promising enterprises have been ruined by straining after large profits, while working with an undue proportion of borrowed money, money which, in times of panic, has been suddenly withdrawn.

The social tendency is shown in the assignment of public money for educational purposes, the passing of the Education Acts, the pressure of public feeling in favor of rate-supported schools, of higher education for all at the public expense. It is shown in the demand for shorter hours of labor; the insistence that all should work; the attempts —at present only by agitation—to enact limits to the accumulation by individuals of land and capital.

And above all the social tendency is shown in the inclination to resort to law for the effecting of the desired changes; in the recognition that social, not individual effort is necessary for the reform of the social system; in the feeling that the continuance of vice and misery side by side with civilisation is intolerable, and that some means must be found to put an end to them.

The problem now set before us is how to eradicate the anti-social, and to cultivate the social, instincts in men and women. Much would be gained if once it were generally recognised that the desire for huge personal accumulation is essentially anti-social, is a survival from the brute. At the present time this desire is veiled under less offensive names, such as "business ability", "sharpness", "energy", etc., etc., but when the veil is stripped away it stands forth in its repulsive nudity. To desire sufficiency, sufficiency for health and pleasure now, and for the time when work-power has failed, that is natural and reasonable; to desire superfluity, superfluity for ostentation and waste, that is barbaric.

Enough for each of work, of leisure, of joy; too little for none; too much for none; such is the Social Ideal. Better to strive after it worthily, and fail, than to die without striving for it at all.

IV.—The Reconcilement of Diverging Interests.

Wherever a school of thought has succeeded in gaining many adherents, and in holding its ground for a considerable period, it is probable that it possesses some truth, or part of some truth, valuable to humanity. Very often it may see only one side of the truth, and so may present a half as though it were the whole; and the bitterest combats are generally waged between those who hold separately the two halves which, united, would form the perfect whole. Truths which are complementary to each other are held as though they were mutually destructive, and those who should be brothers in a common strife turn their weapons against each other's breasts. Such has been the conflict between the "Individualistic" and the "Socialistic" schools; each holds a truth and does well to cling to it, for neither truth could be lost without injury to Society; the whole truth is to be found by joining the twain, for there is needed for the highest humanity the perfecting of the Individual within a highly organised Society.

Looking back for a moment at our Industrial Period, which may be taken as incarnated in the "Manchester School", we shall find that it has given to the world some important information touching production. It has proved that the productiveness of labor can be enormously increased by co-operation and the division of labor; that individual production of the ordinary necessaries of life is a mistake; that it is cheaper to weave cotton goods by machinery than to leave each housekeeper to do her own spinning and weaving. The Manchester School has for ever rendered it impossible that we shall return to general production by "cottage industries": it has proved that large numbers should co-operate in production; that labor should be economised by much division; that machine-made goods should supersede hand-made in large departments of industry; these are the contributions of the Manchester School to progress. With these truths which it taught were bound up errors which raised against it a widespread revolt. Its system appeared as though it were based on the assumption that, while labor was to be co-operative, the profits arising from the associated labor were to go to the enrichment of an individual. It deified competition, and consecrated as its patterns those who could best outwit their rivals and outstrip them in the race for wealth. Its maxim, "buy in the cheapest market and sell in the dearest", while admirable as counsel for money-making, did not always conduce in practice to perfect honesty, and is scarcely sufficient as the end of life. "Get money; by fair means if thou canst, but by all means get money", was a somewhat brutally frank way of putting "business" morality. It tended to regard men too much as mechanical instruments of production, significantly calling men, women, and children "hands", instead of human beings. This school it was of which I spoke on p. 15 as having misused Political Economy, and as having taught as though the laws of Political Economy said "Get rich", instead of stating the conditions of getting rich; they have used it as the science of Mechanics might be used, if instead of teaching by it how a weight may be lifted with least exertion of muscular strength, it were appealed to as declaring that everyone should lift weights.

Turning to the Socialistic School, we find that it enshrines the truth that man is a social animal, and that his progress must lie in the direction of closer social union. Within this school again we find three camps, the Collectivist, the Communistic, and the Anarchist, the latter of which is really tenanted by extreme Individualists, who are separated from the ordinary Individualistic School by their desire to overturn the present social system, and to destroy the "rights of property".

The Socialists have learned from the Manchester School the conditions of wealth-production on a large scale, and seeing that industry as now conducted leads to the enriching of a few and the hopeless poverty of the many, it lays hands on the raw material and the means of production and claims these as collective property. There is, perhaps, among many of us who belong to this school too great an inclination to think that the environment is everything, and to ignore the reaction of the organism on the environment. There is too much forgetfulness of the worse types of men and women, results of the Industrial Period, who would not be suddenly changed even if their environment could be suddenly transformed; there is too reckless a desire to overturn, without asking what curb would be kept, in the general overturning, on the degraded and criminal products of our present civilisation.

The Individualistic School, whether it is carried to the extreme Anarchist position, or maintains the sufficiency of reform along the broad lines of the present social state, brings into prominence the right of individual liberty, and the value of individual initiative. One outside, and one inside, nominal Socialism, each is the result of a dread of, a recoil against, over-much State regulation and State interference. Each lays down the vital truth that free play for human faculties, encouragement not discouragement of variations, are necessary to human progress. Each points out that a perfect State is only possible by the perfecting of individual citizens, and each is apt to lay so much stress on the organism as to overlook the immense importance of the environment. There is, of course, as I have said above, the fundamental difference between the Anarchists and those generally recognised as Individualists, that the former appear to negate, while the latter maintain, the right of private property. I have only put them together as alike in one thing, that they assert the right of the Individual against the State, while the Collectivist Socialist asserts the right of the State as against the Individual.

Pressed on the matter, however, both Individualist and Socialist are found to hold a common object; the Individualist admits that the claims of the unit must yield if they come into conflict with those of Society: the Socialist admits that he is working for a higher social state in order that each individual may have room and opportunity to develop to the highest point of which he is capable. Is there not here a possible reconcilement? Is not the ideal of all good and earnest reformers practically the same, although seen by them from different sides? True, the Individualist is not generally in favor of nationalising the means of production, and herein differs in his method from the Socialist; but is this difference any reason for their posing as antagonists? The difference is not greater than that between the Socialist who secures to the worker the private property he has himself earned, and the Communist who would have all property common; or between the Collectivist and the Anarchist schools. Yet these can work together for common objects, while differing in much; and so should work the Socialist and the Radical Individualist against the common foe, the idle class that lives as parasite on Society.

The first matter on which all agree is that the environment must be largely modified by law. The Socialist will carry this modifying process further than will the Individualist, but here again it is a question between them of degree. Speaking as a Socialist, I desire to see laws passed which will render education tax-supported, compulsory, and secular, so that all the children of the community may receive a common education; which will fix a normal working day; which will render factory inspection more efficient, and extend inspection to shops and rooms of every kind in which employees work; which will enforce sanitary inspection and prevent it from being the farce it now is; which will enable the building of healthy houses, and provide plenty of recreation ground in every town. All these measures are imperatively necessary now, and immediately necessary, in order that the environment may be changed sufficiently for the development of healthier organisms. After a while most of them will not be needed; when all have felt the benefit of education, compulsion to educate will become a dead letter; when labor is better organised, when the words employer and employee shall no longer have any facts answering to them, when all production is for use, not for profit, there will be no need of a law limiting the working day, for none will be driven to over-long labor by the awful pressure of starvation and of fear of future distress. Factory inspection will be a very easy task when there are no longer over-greedy owners trying to wring every possible penny out of their "hands"; and the need for sanitary inspection will pass when there are no slums, and when every householder understands the conditions of health.

The organism, born into and growing up in a healthier environment, will be more vigorous and therefore more capable of evolving a higher individuality, a more marked personality. The evolution of individuality is now checked, in some by poverty and over-hard and prolonged toil, in some by the strict conventions of fashion, in some by the unsuitability of their work to their capacities, in some by a narrow and superstitious education, in all by the unhealthy social atmosphere they are compelled to breathe. The loss to the community by waste of power, due to the crushing out of all individuality among hundreds upon hundreds of thousands, is a loss simply incalculable. When all are fully educated through childhood and youth, the faculties of each developed and trained, then each individual will be able to evolve along his own line, and the full value of each personality will enrich Society. It is often argued that a wide and thorough education will unfit people for the drudgery necessary for supporting the existence of Society, and that "some one"—never the speaker, of course!—must do the "dirty work". There are two lines of answer to the objection. First, education does *not* unfit people for doing any necessary work; it is the ignorant, superficial, "genteel" person who fears that the veneer of polish may rub off in use. The educated brain, brought to bear on manual work, economises labor and minimises drudgery. General education will certainly bring about the substitution of machinery for men and women wherever possible, for doing really unpleasant labor; and ingenuity will be exerted in the invention of labor-saving machinery when educated people find themselves face to face with repulsive kinds of toil. At present they shove off all the unpleasant work on to others: then, all being educated and there being no helot class, means will be found to avoid most of the really disagreeable work. If any such remains, which cannot be done by machinery, those who by doing it serve Society will be honored, not looked down on as they are now; or possibly some minute fraction of it will fall to the lot of each. Secondly, if it were as true as it is false that education unfitted people for "menial" work, no class has the right to keep another class in ignorance and degradation, in order that its own fingers may not be soiled. The answer to the querulous argument: "Who is to light our fires and cook our dinners, when the servants are as good as their masters?" is the very plain one: "You yourself, if you want the things done, and cannot find anyone willing to do those services for you, in exchange for services you are able to do for them." In the coming times everyone will have to do something, and to do some one thing well. We shall not all have to light fires, for the principle of division of labor will come in, but the one who lights the fire will be a free and independent human being, not a drudge. There is no doubt that domestic labor will be very much lessened, when those who enjoy the results can no longer put off all the toil which produces them on some one else. Even now, the work of a house can be wonderfully diminished if a little intelligence be brought to bear upon it, although domestic labor-saving machines are still in their infancy. The great "servant problem" will be solved by the disappearance of servants, the wide introduction of machinery, and the division among the members of each domestic commonwealth of the various necessary duties. The prospect is really not so very terrible when quietly surveyed.

Whither is Society evolving? It is evolving towards a more highly developed individuality of its units, and towards their closer co-ordination. It is evolving towards a more generous brotherhood, a more real equality, a fuller liberty. It is evolving towards that Golden Age which poets have chanted, which dreamers have visioned, which martyrs have died for: towards that new Republic of Man, which exists now in our hope and our faith, and shall exist in reality on earth.

MODERN SOCIALISM.

BY

ANNIE BESANT.

[SECOND EDITION.]

LONDON:
FREETHOUGHT PUBLISHING COMPANY,
63 FLEET STREET, E.C.

1890.

MODERN SOCIALISM.

GREAT changes are long in the preparing, and every thought that meets ultimately with wide acceptance is lying inarticulate in many minds ere it is syllabled out by some articulate one, and stands forth a spoken Word. The *Zeitgeist* has its mouth in those of its children who have brain to understand, voice to proclaim, courage to stand alone. Some new Truth then peals out sonorous and far-sounding as the roll of the thunder, melodious to the ears attuned to the deep grand harmonies of Nature, but terrible to those accustomed only to the subdued lispings of artificial triflers, and the murmurs which float amid the hangings of courtly halls.

When such an event occurs a few hearken, study, and then rejoicingly accept the new Truth; these are its pioneers, its apostles, who go out to proclaim it to the as yet unbelieving world. They meet with ridicule, then with persecution; for ever the new Truth undermines some hoary Lie, which has its band of devoted adherents living on the spoils of its reign. Slowly, against custom and tradition, against selfishness and violence, even against indifference, deadliest foe of all, this band of devoted teachers makes its onward way. And the band grows and grows, and each convert becomes in his turn a pioneer; until at last the victory is won, and the minority has become the majority; and then the time comes for some new Truth once more, and the old struggle is gone over afresh, and so again and again; and thus the race makes progress, and humanity climbs ever upward towards the perfect life.

During the last century and a quarter the social problem has been pressing for solution on all who have brains to think, and hearts to feel. The coexistence of wealth and penury, of idle prodigality and laborious stint; the terrible fact that "progress and poverty" seem to march hand-in-hand; the growing slums in large towns; the huge fortunes and the starving poor; these things make content impossible, and force into prominence the question: "Must this state of things continue? Is there no possible change which will cure, not only palliate, the present evils?"

Great hopes have sprung into being from time to time, each in turn to be blighted. Machinery was to double production and diminish toil, to spread comfort and sufficiency everywhere. It made cotton-lords and merchant-princes with one hand, and with the other created a proletariat unlike aught the world had seen, poor in the midst of the wealth it created, miserable in the midst of luxury, ignorant in the midst of knowledge, savage in the midst of civilisation. When the repeal of the Corn Laws was striven for and accomplished, once more hope rose high. Cheap food was to put an end to starvation. Alas! in the streets of the wealthiest city in Christendom, men and women perish for lack of a loaf of bread.

Nor is this persistence of misery and of squalor the only sign which troubles the brain and the heart of the student of the social problem. He notes the recurring crises in industry, the inflations and depressions of trade. At one time all is prosperous; demand is brisk, and supply can scarce keep pace with it; wages rise, full time is worked, production is enormously increased. Then a change creeps over all; supply has overtaken, has surpassed demand; the market is glutted; the warehouses are filled with unsaleable goods; short time begins; wages fall; mills are closed; furnaces are damped out; many workers are discharged. Then the unemployed in the large towns increase in number; the poor-rate rises; distress spreads upwards. After a while the depression passes; trade improves; and the whole weary circle is trodden once more. Nor is this all; although there has been "over-production" there is want of the necessaries of life; there are unsaleable clothing goods in the warehouses, and half-naked people shivering outside; too many blankets, and children crying themselves to sleep for cold. This monstrous absurdity, of commodities a drug in the market, and human beings perishing for want of those very commodities, stares us ever in the face. Cannot human brain discover some means to put an end to this state of things, a state which would be ludicrous were it not for the horrible suffering involved in it? Some say, this must always be so; that the poor shall be for ever with us; that commercial crises are inevitable; that these evils are not susceptible of complete cure. If this indeed be true, then I know not that any better advice can be given to humanity than that given to Job by his wife, to "curse God and die". But I think not so meanly of human intelligence; I believe not that our present industrial system, little more than a century old, must needs be eternal; I believe that the present system, devised by man and founded in greed of gain, may by man be changed; and that man's growing power over external nature may be used to bring comfort and wealth to each, and not, as now, to enrich the few at the cost of the enslavement of the many.

Various attempts to bring about a better social state have been made by earnest and noble-hearted men during the last hundred years. I leave aside such systems as those of the Moravians, because they cannot be regarded as in any sense schemes for the reconstruction of society. They, like the monastic communities, were merely attempts to create oases, fenced in from the world's evils, where men might prepare for a future life. These efforts were but crude attempts at Communism, and were foredoomed to failure, economic evolution not having reached the point at which a scientific Communism will become possible. With these the name of Robert Owen will be for ever associated.

Owen's first experiment was made at New Lanark, in connexion with the cotton-mills established there by Mr. Dale, his father-in-law. He became the manager of these in 1797, and set himself to work to improve the condition of the operatives and their families. The success which attended his efforts, the changes wrought by education and by fair dealings, encouraged him to plan out a wider scheme of social amelioration. In 1817 he was asked to report on the causes of poverty to the Committee on the Poor Laws, and in this report he dwelt on the serious increase of pauperism which had followed the introduction of machinery, and urged that employment ought to be found for those who were in need of it. He "recommended that every union or county should provide a farm for the employment of their poor; when circumstances admitted of it, there should be a manufactory in connexion with it" ("Robert Owen," by A. J. Booth, p. 70). On the farm, buildings were to be built for housing the laborers, consisting of "a square, divided into two parallelograms by the erection of public buildings in the centre"; these would consist of "a kitchen, mess-room, school-rooms, library and lecture hall. The poor would enjoy every advantage that economy could suggest: the same roof would cover many dwellings: the same stove might warm every room: the food would be cooked at the same time, and on the same fire: the meals would be eaten from the same table, in the society of friends and fellow-workers. Sympathies now restricted to the family would be thus extended to a community: the union would be still further cemented by an equal participation in the profits, an equal share in the toil. . . . . Competition is the cause of many vices; association will be their corrective" (*Ibid*, pp. 70—72). Soon after this report, Mr. Owen published a letter, urging the reconstitution of "the whole of society on a similar basis"; the lowest class was to consist of paupers, to be drafted into the proposed establishments; the second of the "working class"; the third of laborers, artisans, and tradesmen, with property of from £100 to £2,000; the fourth of persons unable or unwilling to work, owning from £1,000 to £20,000; these were to employ the second class. The workman was to be supported by this class in comfort for seven years in exchange for his labor, and then was to be presented by it with £100, so that he might enter class three; if he remained as a worker for five years more he was to have £200.

A community of workers, as recommended by Owen, was started in 1825, under the management of Abraham Combe, at Orbiston, nine miles east of Glasgow, and it began well; but Combe died in 1827, and with his death the whole thing went to pieces. A few months before the settlement at Orbiston, Robert Owen sailed for America, and he purchased a property named Harmony, consisting of 30,000 acres in Indiana, from the Rappites, a religious communistic body. He advertised for inhabitants, and gathered together a mixed crowd; "there were some enthusiasts who had come, at great personal sacrifice, to face a rude life and to mix among rude men, who had no object but to work out the great problem of a New Society; there were others who fancied they could secure abundance with little labor, prepared to shirk their share in the toil, but not to forego their share in the reward" (*Ibid*, p. 106). In the following year, 1826, "New Harmony" inaugurated a system of complete Communism, much against Owen's judgment; a number of small independent communities were soon formed, eight of these having already broken off from New Harmony early in 1827, the difficulties attendant on widely extended common life being found insuperable. In 1828, Robert Owen was forced to confess that his efforts had failed, and that "families trained in the individual system" could not suddenly be plunged into pure Communism with success. It boots not to dwell here on his further efforts in England. Robert Owen's experiments failed, but out of his teaching arose the co-operative movement, and the impulse to seek some rational system of society has, since his time, never quite died out in England.

In America a large number of communities have been established, mostly religious in character. From the careful account given of them by Charles Nordhoff, the following brief details are taken (all numbers relate to 1874). The Amana community consists of 1,450 members; they have a property of 25,000 acres, and live in seven small towns; they are Germans, very pious and very prosperous; their head is a woman, who is directly inspired by God. The Harmony Society, Economy, near Pittsburg, consists of followers of Rapp, who founded the society in 1805. They are all Germans and number 110, in addition to about 100 hired laborers and some sixty children. They live in comfort, and have clearly done well unto themselves, owning now a very large amount of property. The Separatists of Zoar, Ohio, are, once more, Germans: they started in 1817, have now about 300 members, own 7,000 acres of land, and are prosperous exceedingly. The Shakers, established in 1792, are scattered over several States, number about 2,415, own about 100,000 acres of land, are divided into fifty-eight communities, and are wealthy and prosperous; the members are American and English. The Perfectionists of Oneida and Wallingford are American, and the first attempt by them at communal living took place in 1846. They number 521. and own 894 acres of land. They also are prosperous. The Aurora and Bethel Communes, in Oregon, are German, or "Pennsylvania Dutch"; they started in 1844, and now number some 600 persons: their property extends to 23,000 acres, and they live in much comfort. The Icarians, founded by Etienne Cabet in 1848, are nearly all French; they have hitherto been less fortunate than the preceding societies, in consequence of mismanagement at the start; a heavy debt was incurred early in the movement, and members fell off; but a few resolute men and women settled down steadily in Iowa, with 4,000 acres of land, and 20,000 dollars of debt; they had to give up the land to their creditors, but managed to redeem nearly half of it, and they are now 65 in number, own 1,936 acres, have no debts, and have acquired a large live stock. They still live very plainly, but are on their way to prosperity, having conquered all the difficulties amid which they started; their constitution is perfectly democratic and they are without religion. A Swedish community at Bishop Hill, Illinois, was formed by a pietist sect which emigrated to America to escape persecution in 1846-1848. They were terribly poor at first and lived in holes in the ground, with a tent for a church, but gradually acquired property; until in 1859 they owned 10,000 acres of land, worth 300,000 dollars, and some magnificent live stock. Unfortunately their piety led to such extreme dullness that the younger members of the society revolted: debt was incurred, individuality was advocated, the property was divided, and the community ceased to exist. Lastly, there are two small communities, founded in 1871 and 1874; the former, the Progressive Community, at Cedar Vale, consists partly of Russians; it possesses 320 acres of good land, and has only eight members, of whom one is a child. The second, the Social Freedom Community, consists of three adults and three lads, Americans, and has a farm of 333 acres.

The whole of these societies can only be regarded as in the nature of experiments, and as such they are extremely interesting; each community has succeeded in gaining comfort and independence, but these small bodies, living chiefly by agriculture in a thinly-populated country on virgin soil, while they show the advantages of associated labor, really offer no data for the solution of the problems which beset a complex society. They are a return to more primitive forms of living, not an onward social evolution, and they are only possible in a "new country". Further, while they are communistic so far as their own members are concerned, they are individualistic and competitive in their aspect to the outer world; each small group holds its own property, and transacts all its business on the old lines in its dealings with the rest of the nation. This is, of course, inevitable, since each is encircled by competition: but it must not be overlooked that all these organisations, like co-operative societies at home, are nothing more than enlarged families, and are essentially individualistic—winning sufficiency for their own narrow, isolated circles, but leaving untouched the question of national poverty. They are arks, rescuing their inmates from the deluge, but they do nothing to drain away the seething ocean of misery.

Modern Socialism has wider aims than the saving of a few, or the piecemeal reformation of society; it is an attempt to get at the root of the poverty which now prevails; to find out how fortunes are made; why commercial crises occur: what are the real relations of capital and labor at the present time.

In speaking of "fortunes", I do not here include fortunes made by gambling, as on the Stock Exchange. They fall under another category, for in gambling, whether on the Stock Exchange or on the card table, wealth is not really made: it only passes from one pocket to another. The gambler, or the burglar, may "make a fortune" so far as he is himself concerned; but it is not done by the creation of wealth, but only by transferring wealth already existing from the pocket of its temporory possessor into his own; in both businesses the profits are large because the risks are great, and the penalty for failure heavy for the moment.

Socialism, as an industrial system, is chiefly concerned with fortunes in the making, with the way in which the wealth created by associated labor passes into the hands of individuals who do little or nothing in exchange for it. These fortunes arise from the ownership of the instruments of production, or of the raw material out of which wealth is to be manufactured; from the ownership, that is, of capital or of land.

Production.

Let us take the case of the possessor of capital employed in manufacture. This man desires to obtain more wealth than he can produce alone, more than he can individually produce even with the help of machinery. He must consequently hire others, who, in exchange for a certain fixed sum to be paid to them by him, shall allow him to take over the whole results of their labor, and to pocket the difference between those results and the fixed sum paid by him. This fixed sum is known as wage, and is "the market price of labor". We have therefore here two classes face to face with each other: one is a class which is the owner of capital, that is which possesses the instruments of production; the other is a class which possesses the labor force, without which the instruments of production are useless, but which must perish if it cannot get hold of some of those instruments. (Behind the capitalists is a third-class, the land-owning, with which the capitalist has to come to terms: that will be dealt with afterwards.) This second class stands therefore at this disadvantage; that while the capitalist can, if he pleases, utilise his own labor-force for his own subsistence, it cannot subsist at all except with his consent and aid, being shut out from the raw material by the landowner, and from the instruments of production by himself. Put a naked man on fertile soil in a decent climate and he will subsist; he will live on fruits and berries while with his hands he fashions some rough tool, and with the help thereof makes him a better one out of the raw material he will form an instrument of production with those original instruments of production given him by nature, his fingers and the muscles of his body; then with his instrument and the raw material at his feet he will labor and win his livelihood. But in our complex society this opening is not before him; the raw material is enclosed and trespassers are prosecuted; if he picks fruit for food, he is a thief; if he breaks off a bough to make a rough tool, he is arrested; he cannot get an instrument of production, and if he could he would have nothing to use it on; he has *nothing* but his labor-force, and he must either sell that to someone who wants it, or he must die. And the sale must be complete. His labor force is bought for so much down per week or per month; it no longer belongs to himself, it is owned by his master, and he has not any right over that which it produces; he has sold it, and if he wants to resume possession he must give notice of his wish to the owner thereof; having resumed possession it is of no use to him; he can only live by selling it to somebody else. He is "free", in so far that he is able to change his master: he is a slave in that he must sell the labor force in his body for food. The man whose labor-force has been sold to another for life is regarded by all as a slave; the man whose labor-force is sold for stated terms is regarded by most as free; yet in comparing the conditions of the two, it is well to bear in mind that the slave, in becoming a chattel, becomes of value to his master, and it is the interest of the latter to feed him well and to keep up his physical strength as long as is possible; also in old age he is fed and housed, and can die in peace amid his fellows. Whereas the wage earner has no such value, but it is his master's interest to get as much work out of him as is possible, without regard for his health, there being plenty to take his place when he is worn out; and when he is old, he is separated from wife and child and is left to die in the prison we call a workhouse. The slave is valuable, as the horse and the ox are valuable, to his owner: the wage-earner is valuable only as a garment, which is cast into the dusthole when it is worn out.

It may be answered that the wage-earner by good fortune, industry, and thrift, may be able so to save of his earnings that he may escape the workhouse, and may even himself become independent and an "employer of labor". True. So might a lucky slave become free. But the truth that some may rise out of their class does not render satisfactory the state of the class, and the very fact that such rising is held out as a reward and a stimulus is an admission that an escape from the proletariat must be the natural longing of every proletarian. The rising of a few does not benefit the proletariat as a whole, and it is the existence of this unpropertied proletariat which is the evil thing.

To this proletariat, waiting to sell its labor-force, the capitalist goes, for it is here that he will be able to obtain the wealth-making strength which he requires. The next question is: What determines the wage which he is to pay? That is: what fixes the market price of labor-force?

acting on one side temporary and comparatively trivial causes which may slightly affect it one way or the other, there are two constant determinants: population, and standard of living. The market-price of labor-force will largely depend on the quantity of labor-force in the market; if the supply exceed the demand, the price will be low; if the demand exceed the supply, the price will go up. If an employer requires fifty laborers, and two hundred laborers compete with each other for the employment he offers, and if the employment stands between them and starvation, he will be able to beat down their price until it touches the lowest point at which they can subsist. The more rapid the multiplication of the proletariat, the better for the capitalist class.

The other determinant is the "standard of living" or "standard of comfort". Wage can never sink beyond the point at which a man and his family can temporarily exist thereon; this is the extreme limit of its fall, inasmuch as a man will not work unless he can exist on the results of his work. As a matter of fact, it does not often sink so low; the wage of an ordinary operative is more than barely suffices to keep him and his family alive, but large numbers of the laboring poor are habitually underfed, and are liable to the diseases brought on by low living, as well as to premature aging and death arising from the same cause. It is a significant fact that the deathrate of the poor is much higher than the deathrate of the rich. Wage is lower in countries in which the standard of living is low, than in those in which it is, by comparison, higher. Thus in parts of Scotland, where oatmeal is much used for food, and children run much barefoot, wage is normally lower than in England, where wheaten flour and shoes and stockings are expected. Any general lowering of the standard of living is therefore to be deprecated—as the wide substitution of cheap vegetable food-stuffs for more expensive articles of diet. The standard of living also (and chiefly, in any given country) affects wages through its effect on population. Mill points out ("Principles of Political Economy," Book II, chap. xi, sec. 2) that "wages do adapt themselves to the price of food", either (*a*) from children dying prematurely when food rises, and wages were before barely sufficient to maintain them, or (*b*) from voluntary restriction of the growth of population when the laborers refuse to sink below a certain standard of living. In each case the diminution of labor supply causes a rise of wage. "Mr. Ricardo", says Mill, "considers these two cases to comprehend all cases. He assumes that there is everywhere a minimum rate of wages: either the lowest with which it is physically possible to keep up the population, or the lowest with which the people will choose to do so. To this minimum he assumes that the general rate of wages always tends; that they can never be lower, beyond the length of time required for a diminished rate of increase to make itself felt, and can never long continue higher." This is the "iron law of wages", and it is the recognition of its truth which, among other reasons, sets Socialists against the wage-system of industry. [It must not be forgotten that the phrase "ordinary operative" does not include all the workers. There is a large class which obtains barely subsistence wage, and those who are not regularly employed are on the very verge of starvation. The hard lot of these must not be left out of sight in impeaching the present social state.]

The capitalist, then, buys as much labor-force as he desires, or as his means allow, at the market price, determined in the way we have seen. This labor-force he proposes to utilise for his own advantage; with some of his capital he buys it; some of his capital consists in machinery, and the labor-force set at work on this machinery is to produce wealth. The labor-force and the instruments of production are now brought together; they will now produce wealth, and both they and the wealth they produce are the property of the capitalist.

Our next inquiry is: Where does the capitalist look for his profit? He has bought machinery; he has bought labor-force; whence comes the gain he is seeking? The profit of the capitalist must arise from the difference between the price he pays for labor-force and the wealth produced by it; out of this difference must be paid his rent, the loss incurred by wear-and-tear, and the price of the raw material on which his machinery works; these provided for, the remainder of the difference is his "profit". The analysis of the way in which this profit arises is, then, the task that comes next.

In Karl Marx's "Das Capital" may be found a carefully

elaborated exposition of "surplus-value". The student will do well to read his seventh chapter, on the "production of use-value and surplus-value"; in reading, he must remember Marx's definitions of value and use-value, which of course govern the whole. Value is human labor incorporated in a commodity; use-value is that which in a commodity satisfies some human want. The "use-value" of Marx is identical with the "intrinsic natural worth" of Locke. Locke says: "The intrinsic natural worth of any thing consists in its fitness to supply the necessities, or serve the conveniences of human life". ("Considerations of the Lowering of Interest," etc, Locke's Works, vol. ii., p. 28, ed. 1777). As an instance of the production of surplus-value—that is of the difference between the capital which the capitalist expends in production and that which he possesses when the production is complete—Marx takes the case of the manufacture of ten pounds of thread. The capitalist buys ten pounds of cotton at 10s.; wear-and-tear of machinery in the spinning of the cotton into thread raises his expenditure to 12s.; further, six hours of work are necessary to turn the ten pounds of cotton into ten pounds of thread.

Now suppose that a man in six hours is able to produce sufficient to maintain himself for a day;—that is that he produces as much as might be exchanged for a day's consumption of the necessaries of life. Let us value this at 3s. in money. That 3s. which is the monetary equivalent of his six hours' labor must be added to the cost of production of the thread; its value has therefore risen finally to 15s. If the capitalist now sells his ten pounds of thread for 15s., he will only receive back as much as he has expended; he will have made no profit. But suppose the working day be of twelve hours instead of six, the wages paid will none the less be fixed at 3s. by the standard of living; but in that second six hours the operative can transform another ten pounds of cotton into another ten pounds of thread; as before, cotton and wear-and-tear will amount to 12s.; but these ten pounds of thread have a value of 15s. as had the previous ten pounds although they have only cost the capitalist 12s. Hence the final product of the day's labor has a value of 30s., but has cost the capitalist only 27s. The value added by the operative in the second six hours has brought *him* no equivalent; it is "surplus-value", value added by him over the value whose equivalent he receives in wage; this creation of surplus-value is the aim of the capitalist.

Now, without tying ourselves down to the exact figures and the phraseology of Marx, we may yet see by a little thought that his main position is essentially correct. If a capitalist buys £1 worth of raw material; if his machinery is depreciated say by the value of one shilling in working up the raw material; if he pays in wage 5s. for the labor-force expended on it; he will most certainly not be content with selling the finished product for 26s. He demands a "profit" on the transaction, and this profit can only be the difference between that which is paid to labor, and the value, in the ordinary sense of the word, which labor creates.

It is sometimes objected that nothing is gained by Marx's divisions of "value", "surplus value", and "exchange value", but that, on the contrary, they transport economics into a metaphysical region away from the solid ground of facts. It is urged that it is better to represent the conditions thus: that the worker produces a mass of commodities; that the capitalist sells these commodities for what they will fetch in the market, the price being fixed, not by the duration of the labor embodied in them, but by the relative utilities of money and commodity to buyer and seller; that the capitalist gives over to the producer sufficient of the results of the sale to enable the producer to exist, and pockets the remainder. This presentment is a statement of the facts as they are; Marx's "value" is a metaphysical abstraction corresponding to nothing existing at the present time, however true it would be under ideal conditions. The main point to grasp, however, is obvious, whichever of these presentments is thought preferable. Capital, under our present industrial system, is the result of unpaid labor—a matter to be further considered later in this essay. But it must be remembered that, as a matter of fact, the profit made by the capitalist is not a fixed quantity, as is the "surplus value" of Marx; but that the capitalist not only preys on the worker, but also on the necessities of the consumer, his profit rising and falling with the changes of demand and supply. The phrase "surplus value", if it is to be retained at all, might well be extended to cover the whole difference between the price paid to labor for the commodities it produces, and the price obtained for those commodities by the capitalist employer of labor. It is in this wide sense that the phrase is used in the following pages, not in the metaphysical sense of Marx.

We are now in a position to understand how large fortunes are made, and why Capital and Labor are ever at war.

Before the commencement of the Industrial Period—which may be fairly dated from the invention of the Spinning Jenny in 1764—it was not possible to accumulate great wealth by the employment of hired labor. By hand-work, or by the use of the very simple machines available prior to that date, a single operative was not able to produce sufficient to at once support himself and to largely enrich others. "Masters and men" consequently formed a community of workers, without the sharp divisions that now exist between capitalist and "hands"; and the employer would have been as much ashamed of *not* working deftly at his trade, as the son of a Lancashire cotton-lord would be ashamed if he were suspected of throwing a shuttle in one of his father's looms. Under these conditions there was very little surplus-value to be absorbed, and there were consequently no great aggregations of the purely industrial classes. The introduction of machinery multiplied enormously the productive power of the operative, while it did not increase the wage he received. A man receiving 3s. for a day of twelve hours, produced, we will say for the sake of illustration, surplus-value to the amount of 1s.; after the introduction of machinery he received the same wage and produced an enormously increased surplus-value. Thus the fortunes of the lucky possessors of the new machinery rose by "leaps and bounds"; lads who began at the loom were owners of palaces by middle age; even later on, after the first rush had spent itself, I have myself met Lancashire cotton-lords who were mill-hands in their youth; but most certainly their wealth had only been made by the results of the toil of many becoming concentrated in the hands of one.

Another step was taken to increase surplus-value. Depending, as it does, on the difference between the value produced by the worker and the amount paid to him as wage, it is obvious that if it be possible to obtain the same amount of produce from purchased labor-force while reducing the purchase-money, the surplus-value will become larger. This step was soon taken, for it was found that many machines could be superintended by a woman quite as effectively as by a man, while female labor-force was purchasable in the market at a lower rate. Hence the large introduction of female "hands" into cotton mills, and as married women were found more "docile" than unmarried—docility increasing with the number of mouths crying for bread at home—there came the double curse on the producers, of male labor being pushed aside by female labor at lower wage, and of untidy home and neglected children, bereft of mother's care. Yet another step. Child-labor was cheaper even than woman-labor, and by utilising children with their pitiful wage, surplus-value might be swollen to yet larger proportions; and as wives had fought with husbands for wage, so children now fought with fathers and mothers, until verily a man's foes in the labor-market were they of his own household.

There was, however, a way of increasing surplus-value apart from the amount of daily wage. The lengthening of the hours of labor has obviously the same result in this respect as the lowering of wage. The very zenith of the production of surplus-value, the most complete exploitation of the producers, the perfect triumph of the capitalist ideal of free contract and of *laissez-faire*, were reached when little children, at nominal wage, were worked from fifteen to sixteen hours a day, and princely fortunes were built up by human sacrifice to the devil of greed, in fashion that shall never, so help us tongue, and pen, and arm, be again possible in this fair English land.

We have at the present time no exact figures available which can enable us to judge of the precise amount of surplus value produced in the various departments of industry. In America, the Bureaus of Labor Statistics help us, and from these we learn some suggestive facts.

	Average wage paid to worker.	Extra net value produced by worker.		Average wage paid to worker.	Extra net value produced by worker.
1850	£49 12	£41 16	1870	£62 0	£69 0
1860	58 8	65 10	1880	69 4	64 14

(Taken from Laurence Gronlund's quotation of these

returns in his "Co-operative Commonwealth", chap. i. The same figures, as regards total net produce and wages paid, have appeared in a capitalist work.) We have now in England a Labor Bureau somewhat similar to those now existing in the United States, but it is still too young to give us the figures we need. For this Bureau we have to thank Charles Bradlaugh, M.P., who succeeded in passing a resolution in favor of the official publication of similar statistics through the House of Commons. Among the many priceless services he has done to the workers, the obtaining of these is by no means the least. Exact knowledge of the present state of things is a necessary precedent of organic change, and the figures supplied by the Labor Bureau will give us the very weapons that we need.

The absolutely antithetical interests of Capital and Labor have necessitated—and must continue to necessitate while the present system lasts—a constant and embittered war. As Capital can only grow by surplus value, it strives to lengthen the working day and to decrease the daily wage. Labor struggles to shorten the hours of toil, and to wring from Capital a larger share of its own product in the form of higher wage. While Capital is the possession of one class, and Labor is the only property of the other, this strife must go on. There can never be industrial peace until this root of war be pulled up, and until Capital, under the control of the community, shall be used for the fertilisation, instead of for the oppression of Labor.

Since large fortunes are made by manufacturers, and there is no source of wealth save labor applied to natural objects, it is clear that these fortunes are due to the fact that the manufacturers are able to become the owners of the means of production and of labor-force; even these very means of production, with which the present labor-force works, are but past labor-force crystallised. The wage-earners must produce sufficient to maintain themselves from day to day and to increase the capital of the wage-payers, else they will not be employed. Hence arises another evil, the waste of productive force. Men are not employed because their labor-force, embodied in the necessaries of life, will spread sufficiency and comfort throughout the community. They are only employed when the articles produced can be *sold at a profit* by a third party; their products, fairly exchanged for the products of their fellow-laborers—woven cloth, say, for shoes—would clothe warmly the shivering population; but above the cloth produced by the one, and the shoes produced by the other, stand the capitalists, who demand profit for themselves ere the cloth shall be allowed to shield the naked back, or the shoes keep off the pavement the toes blued by the frost. If the employment fails, the wage-earner is out of food; but the erstwhile wage-payer has the capital made by the former to live upon, while its maker starves. The capitalist, truly, cannot increase his capital, unless he can buy labor-force; but he can live on his capital. On the other hand the labor-force must perish unless it can find a purchaser. Let us put the position plainly, for as the great majority of people think the arrangement a perfectly fair one, there is no need to cover it over with a veil of fine phrases and roundabout expressions. The owner of raw material and of the means of production faces the unpropertied proletarian, and says to him: "I hold in my hands the means of existence; unless you can obtain the means of existence you will die; but I will only let you have them on one condition. And that is that you shall labor for me as well as for yourself. For each hour that you spend in winning bread, you shall spend another in enriching me. I will give you the right to win a hard existence by your labor, if you will give me the right to take whatever you produce beyond that bare existence. You are perfectly free to choose; you can either accept my terms, and let me live on your work, or you can refuse my terms, and starve." Put so baldly, the proposition has a certain brutality in it. Yet when we Socialists argue that a system is bad which concentrates the means of existence in the hands of a propertied class, and leaves an unpropertied class under the hard condition of winning only the right to exist on such terms as may be granted by the propertied; when we urge this, we are told that we are incendiaries, thieves, idiots, or, at the mildest, that our hopes of freeing these enslaved ones are dreams, mere castles in the air.

We have now reached the foundation of modern Socialism. We say: As long as the industrial classes are divided into capitalists and proletarians, so long must continue the present strife, and the present extremes of wealth and of poverty. It is not a mere modification, but a complete revolution of the industrial system which is required. Capital must be controlled by labor, instead of controlling it. The producers must obtain possession of their own product, and must regulate their own labor. The present system has been weighed in the balances and found wanting, and on the wall of the capitalist banqueting-room is written by the finger of modern thought, dipped in the tears and in the bloody sweat of the over-tasked proletariat: "Man hath numbered thy kingdom and finished it. It is divided among the myriads thou hast wronged."

Competition.

Strife is the normal condition of the whole industrial world; Capital strives against Labor, and Labor against Capital, lock-outs and strikes being the pitched battles of the struggle; capitalists strive against capitalists for profits, and the list of the vanquished may be read in the bankruptcy court; workers strive against workers for wage, and injure their own order in the fratricidal combat. Everywhere the same struggle, causing distress, waste, hatred, in every direction; brothers wronging brothers for a trifling gain; the strong trampling down the weak in the frantic race for wealth. It is the struggle of the wild beasts of the forest transferred to the city; the horrible struggle for existence, only in its "civilised" form hearts are wrenched and torn instead of limbs.

It is constantly urged that competition is advantageous because it develops capacity, and by the struggle it causes it brings about the survival of the fittest. The allegation may be traversed on two grounds: granting that capacity is developed by struggle, it is yet developed at great cost of suffering, and it would be more worthy of reasoning beings to seek to bring about the capacity and to avoid the suffering; to borrow an illustration which suggests itself by the very word "struggle", we know that actual fighting develops muscle, endurance, readiness of resource, quickness of the senses; none the less do we regard war as a disgrace to a civilised people, and we find that the useful capacities developed by it may be equally well developed in the gymnasium and the playing-field, without the evils accompanying war. So may education take the place of competition in developing useful qualities. Further we deny that "the fittest" for social progress survive in the competitive struggle. The hardest, the keenest, the most unscrupulous survive, because such are the fittest for the brutal strife; but the generous, the magnanimous, the just, the tender, the thoughtful, the sympathetic, the very types in whose survival lies the hope of the race, are crushed out. In fact, competition *is* war, and the very reasons which move us to endeavor to substitute arbitration for war, should move us to endeavor to substitute co-operation for competition.

But it is urged, competition among capitalists is advantageous to the public, and it is shown that where two or three railway lines compete for custom, the public is better served than where there is only one. Granted. There is an old adage which says that "when thieves fall out, honest men come by their own"; none the less is it better to stop thieving, than to encourage it under the hope that the thieves may fall out, and some of the stolen goods be recovered. So long as capitalists are permitted to exploit labor, so long is it well that they should compete with each other and so have their profits lessened; but it would be still better to stop the exploitation. Accepting the railway instance, it may be rejoined that the German State railways have comfortable carriages that can hold their own against all comers, and that whereas a railway company, eager for dividends, can only be forced into providing decent carriages by fear of losing customers to a rival, a State railway is managed for the benefit of the public, and improvements are readily introduced. Our post-office system shows how improvements are made without any pressure of competition; it has given us cheaper postage, cheaper telegraphing, and is giving us cheaper parcel-delivery; so that we can send from London a letter to Wick for a penny, a telegram thither for sixpence, and a parcel for threepence. It is a matter of pride to the Postmaster-General of the day, as a public servant, to improve his department, although he is protected by law (save in case of parcels only just undertaken) from competition.

Even some economists who approve of competition see the need of limiting its excesses. Mr. R. S. Moffat, for instance, approves of it and thinks that "competition is not only the best, but the only practical means of meeting" "the conflicting natural conditions, between the exigencies of an unknown demand and the fluctuations of an uncertain supply", "that ever has been, or is ever likely to be discovered" ("The Economy of Consumption", p. 114, ed. 1878.) Yet Mr. Moffat points out that "the material cost of competition includes two items: first, superfluous production, or wasted labor; and secondly ill-balanced distribution, or misdirected labor" (p. 115); and he declares: "not content with promoting a healthful industry, it enforces tyrannous laws upon labor, and exacts from the free laborer an amount of toil which the hardest taskmaster never succeeded in wringing from the slave. It disturbs by its excesses the balance of industry which its moderation had established. In times of prosperous production it accumulates stocks till they become a nuisance and a source of the most serious embarrassment to producers, who do not know where to turn for employment to their productive resources; and in adverse times it gambles with them, and deprives consumption of their support at the very time for which they were provided" (pp. 116, 117). "It is upon laborers", he says, "not only as individuals, but as a class, that the great burden of over-production falls" (p. 190.)

I propose to consider I., the evils of competition; II., the remedy proposed by Socialism.

I.—THE EVILS.—Many of these lie on the surface; others become palpable on very slight investigation. They affect the capitalist manufacturer; the distributor; the consumer; and the producing classes.

An ingenious capitalist sees a want and devises an article to meet it; or he devises an article and sets to work to create the want. He places his article before the public, and a demand for it arises. The article either supplies a real want, or it becomes "the fashion", and the demand increases and outstrips the supply. Other capitalists rush in to compete for the profit which is to be made; capital flows rapidly into the particular industry concerned; high wages are offered; operatives flock to it; the supply swells until it overtops the demand. But when this point is touched, the supply is not at once lessened; so long as there is any hope of profit, the capitalists manufacture; wage is lessened to keep up the profit, but this expedient fails; short hours are worked; at last the market becomes thoroughly overstocked. Then distress follows, and while capital seeks new outlets, the operatives fall into the great army of unemployed; and very often the small capitalists, who went into the rush just when profit was at its highest, and who have not sufficient capital to hold out against the fall, and to await a rise, meet the fate of earthenware pots, carried down a torrent among iron ones. When this happens, the result of their speculative folly is held up as an example of the "risks run by capitalists". Nor is this the only way along which a small capitalist sometimes travels to the bankruptcy court. He often borrows money "to extend his business", and if the business shrinks instead of expanding, he becomes bankrupt. In the universal war, the big capitalist fish devour the small fry.

And, after all, even the "successful man" of our competitive society is not one whose lot is to be envied by the healthy human being. Not for him the pure joy in natural beauty, in simple amusements, in intellectual triumph, which is the dower of those unstained by the fight for gold. For the successful competitor in commercial war Nature has no laurel-crown. He has bartered himself for a mess of pottage, and his birthright of healthy humanity is gone from him for evermore. Well does Moffat write his fate: "The man who strives to make a fortune contemplates his own ease and enjoyment, not the good of society. He flatters himself that through his superior skill, tact, wisdom, energy, or whatever quality it is he thinks himself twice as strong in as his neighbors, he will be able to do in half a lifetime what it takes them their whole lives to do. For this he toils and sacrifices his health; for this he rushes upon reckless speculations, and hazards his character and reputation; for this he makes himself indifferent to the rights and callous to the feelings of others; for this he is sordid, mean, and parsimonious. All these are the means by which, according to different temperaments, the same end is pursued. And what is the end? An illusion, nay, worse, a dishonesty. The man who pursues a fortune is not qualifying himself for any other course of life besides that which he at present lives. He is merely striving to escape from duty into enjoyment. And the fever of the strife frequently becomes his whole existence; so that when he has obtained his object, he finds himself unable to do without the excitement of the struggle" (p. 220). Surely in judging the merits of a system it is fair to take into account the injuries it works to its most successful products. Its masterpieces are the withered and dehumanised; its victims are the paupers and the suicides.

Nor can we leave out of account in studying competitive production the waste of material, and of the time spent in working it up, which result from over-production. The accumulation of stock while the demand is lessening means the making and storing of unneeded wares. Some of these are forced into the market, some lie idly in the great warehouses. The retail dealers find themselves overstocked, their shelves laden with unsaleable goods. These fade, and spoil, and rust away—so much good material wasted, so much human labor spent for nought, monuments of a senseless system, of the barbarous, uncalculating blindness of our productive force.

More heavily yet than on the capitalist does competition press on the distributor. A dozen traders compete for the custom which one could satisfactorily supply. The competition for shops in a thickly populated neighborhood drives up the rent, and so adds to the retailer's burden. He is compelled to spend large sums in advertising, striving by brilliancy of color or eccentricity of design to impress himself on the public mind. An army of commercial travellers sweeps over the country, each man with his hand against his neighbor in the same trade, pushing, haggling, puffing his own, depreciating his rival's wares. These agents push their goods on the retailer, often when no real demand for them is coming from the public, and then the retailer puffs them, to create a demand for his supply. Nor must we omit from notice the enormous waste of productive energy in this army of canvassers, advertisers, bill-posters, multiplied middlemen of every kind. The distributive work done by these is absurdly out of proportion to their number. We see several carriers' carts half-filled, instead of half the number filled; each carrier has to deliver goods over the whole of a wide area, so that a man may have to drive five miles to deliver a single parcel at a house a stone's throw from a rival office. Yet each man must receive his full day's wage, and must be paid for the hours he is compelled to waste, as well as for those he spends in useful work. It is the same thing in every business. Three or four carts of each trade go daily down each road, covering the same ground, supplying each one house here and one there, losing time, wearing out horses and traps, a foolish shameful waste. And all those unnecessary distributors are consumers when they might be producers, and are actually making unnecessary work for others as well as for themselves.

Short-sighted people ask: Would you add all these to the crowds of half-starving unemployed now competing for work? No, we answer. We would not add them to the *un*employed; it is only in a system of complete competitive anarchy that there could be unemployed labor on the one hand, and people clamoring for the necessaries of life on the other. We have already seen that under the present system men are only employed where some profit can be made out of them by the person who hires them. Under a saner system there would be none unemployed while the food and clothing supply was insufficient, and the turning of non-productive consumers into productive ones would only mean shorter hours of labor, since the labor necessary to supply the consumption of the population would be divided among a larger number than before. If wealth be the result of labor applied to raw material, poverty may come from the pressure of population on the raw material which limits the means of subsistence, but never from the greater part of the population working to produce wealth on raw material sufficient for their support.

On the consumer falls much of the needless additional expense of advertisements, canvassers, and the rest. The flaming advertisements we see on the walls we pay for in the price of the puffed articles we buy. The trader feels their burden, and tries to recoup himself by adding a fraction of it to the price of the goods he sells. If he is forced to lower his nominal prices in consequence of the pressure of competition with his rivals, yet by adulteration he can really raise, while he seems to lower, them. The nominal width of fabrics does not correspond with the real; woollen goods are sold of which the warp is cotton; tobacco is sold damped unfairly to increase its weight; sand is mixed with sugar; lard or dripping with butter;

chicory with coffee; sloe-leaves with tea; turnip with orange in marmalade; foreign meat is offered as home-grown; damaged flesh is chopped up for sausages; until, at last, as Moffat caustically remarks: "It is not rogues and vagabonds alone who have recourse in trade to expedients which could not be justified by a strict theoretical morality. When this incline is entered upon, there is no resting upon it. Morality itself becomes subject to competition; and the conventional standard of trade morality gets lower and lower, until the things done by respectable people can hardly be distinguished from those done by people who are not respectable, except by the respectability of the people who do them" (p. 154). And in all this adulteration the consumer suffers in health, comfort, and temper. Not only does he pay more than he should for what he buys, but he buys a good deal more than he pays for.

Heaviest of all is the burden on the operative classes, and they suffer in a double character, both as consumers and producers. As consumers, they share the general injury; as producers, their case is yet more serious. If they are in work, their wages are driven down by the competition for employment; they are the first to feel a lessening demand in lengthened hours, in lower wage; as the depression goes on, they are thrown out of work; illness not only incapacitates them for the time, but their place is filled up, while they lie helpless, by the eager waiters for hire; when they combine to strike for fairer treatment, the fringe of unemployed labor around is used against them by the employers; the lowest depth is reached by the crowd who at the dockyard gates at the East of London literally fight for a place in which the foreman's eye may fall on them, and out of the struggling hundreds units are taken on for the day at miserable wage for heavy exhausting work, to be turned out at night to undergo a similar struggle next morning.

The only classes who gain by competition are the big capitalists and the landlords. The big capitalists engaged in manufacture gain by the crushing out of their smaller rivals, and by their ability to hold over stocks produced when wages are low until prices are high. Capitalists who only lend out money on usury, and live on the interest thereby obtained, flourish when the demand for money is brisk. Most of all do landlords, who live on rent, profit by the struggle. In a growing neighborhood rents of commercial premises rise rapidly, and the shopkeeper finds himself heavily taxed by the landlord, who imposes on him practically a graduated income-tax for his own advantage. Thus the chief gainers by competition are the idlers who are permitted to hold the nation's soil, and who live in luxury on the toilers, laughing to see how the fratricidal struggles of those who labor turn to the advantage of those who lounge. And so the strain of living constantly increases for the one class, while the luxury and ostentation of those who levy tax on toil become ever greater, and more aggressive by the contrast.

II. The Remedy.—These evils can be radically cured only in one way; it is by the substitution of co-operation for competition, of organisation for anarchy in industry. The relation of employer and employed must disappear, and a brotherhood of workers, associated for facilitation of production for use, must replace the band of servants toiling for the enrichment of a master by profit. The full details of socialised industry cannot be drawn at length; but it is not difficult to see that the already existent co-operative societies offer a suggestive model, and the trades unions a sufficiently competent means for change. Probably each industry in each district will organise itself, and own, for use, all its means of production; thus the miners of Durham, for instance, organised in their lodges, with their central executive, would form the mining trade society of that district; all the mines of that district would be under their control, and they would elect their officers of all grades. So with all mining districts throughout the land. These separate trade societies would be federated, and a General Board elected by all. The elements of such a self-organised industry exist at the present time, and the more closely the miners can band themselves into district unions, and the unions into a national federation, the more prepared will they be to play their part in the great industrial revolution. It is probable that something of the nature of the royalties now paid to the individual mine-owners will be paid into the National Exchequer, in exchange for the right to work the national soil. A similar organisation would be needed for each productive industry, and probably representatives of each separate industry would form a central Industrial Board. But, I repeat, these details cannot now be laid down authoritatively, any more than the details of the present industrial competitive system could have been laid down before the Industrial Period. On these details Socialists would inevitably differ considerably at the present time, and no special scheme can be fairly stamped as "Socialist" to the exclusion of the rest. But on this main principle all Socialists are agreed: that the only rightful holders of capital are industrial groups, or one great industrial group—the State, *i.e.*, the organised community; that while individuals may hold private property for use, none should hold capital—that is *wealth employed in production*—for individual profit; that while each may have property to consume and to enjoy, none should be allowed to use property to enslave his neighbor, to force another to work for his advantage.

The revolution of distribution will be as great as that in production, and here again co-operation must take the place of competition. We already see the beginnings of a distributive change in the establishment of huge stores for the supply of all the necessaries of life, and the way in which these are crushing out the smaller retail shops. Housewives find it more convenient to go to the single building, than to trudge wearily from shop to shop. Goods bought in very large quantities can be sold more cheaply than if bought in small, and economy, as well as convenience, attract the purchaser to the store. At present these stores are founded by capitalists and compete for custom, but they are forerunners of a rational distributive system. The very enmity they create in the minds of the small traders they ruin is paving the way for the community to take them over for the general advantage. Under Socialism all goods manufactured by the producers would be distributed to the central store of each district; from this central store they would be distributed to the retail stores. Anyone who thinks such distribution impossible had better study the postal system now existing; we do not have post-offices jostling each other as do baker's and butcher's shops: there are sufficient of them for the requirements of the district, and no more. The letters for a town are delivered at the General Post Office; they are sorted out and delivered at the subordinate offices;

the distribution of the correspondence of millions is carried on by a Government Department, quietly, effectively, without waste of labor, with celerity and economy. But then in the Post Office co-operation has replaced competition, organisation has replaced anarchy. Such a system, one hundred years ago, would have been pronounced impossible as the Conservative minds of to-day pronounce impossible its extension to anything except letters and telegrams and parcels. I look for the time when the success of the Post Office will be repeated—and improved—in every department of distribution.

Capital.

We have already seen that Capital is accumulated by withholding from the producer a large part of the value he produces, and we have now to look more closely into the growth of Capital and the uses to which it is put. A glance over the historical Past, as well as the study of the Present, inform us that Capital has always been—as indeed it always must be—obtained from unpaid labor, or, if the phrase be preferred, by the partial confiscation of the results of labor. In communities the economic basis of which was slave-labor, this fact was obvious; the owner confiscated the whole products of his slaves' toil, and he became a capitalist by this process of continued confiscation; while the slave, fed, clothed, and housed out of the fruit of his own labor by his master, never owned anything as of right, nor had any property in that which he created. As civilisation advanced, serf-labor replaced slave-labor; here also the confiscation of the results of labor was obvious. The serf was bound to give so many days of work to his lord without payment; this service rendered, the remainder of his time was his own, to produce for his own subsistence; but the lord's capital increased by the confiscation of the results of the serf's labor during the days whereon he worked for his lord. In modern times "free labor" has replaced serf-labor, but in the present industrial system as truly as in slave and in serf communities, Capital results from unpaid labor, though now from the unpaid labor of the wage-earner. We may search the whole world over, and we shall find no source of wealth save labor applied to natural agents. Wealth is never rained down from heaven, nor is it ever a spontaneous growth; unless indeed wild fruits taken for food be counted wealth, and even to these must human labor be applied in the form of picking ere they can be used. It is the result of human labor; and if one man has more than he has produced, it necessarily follows that another man has less than he has produced. The gain of one must be the loss of another. There are but sixteen court cards in the fifty-two, and if by ingenious shuffling, packing, and dealing, all the court cards fall to one player, only the lower cards can remain for the others.

Separating "Capital" from "Wealth" we may conveniently define it as "wealth devoted to purposes of profit", and as "wealth is the result of labor applied to raw material", Capital becomes the result of labor devoted to purposes of profit. John Stuart Mill says the "accumulated stock of the produce of labor is termed Capital". Macleod: "Capital is any Economic Quantity used for the purpose of Profit". Senior: "Economists are agreed that *whatever* gives a profit is properly called Capital". Something more, however, than the activity of labor is implied in the existence of Capital. There must have been saving, as well as production. Hence Marshall speaks of Capital as "the result of labor and abstinence"; Mill of Capital as "the result of saving"; and so on. It is obvious that if the products of labor were consumed as fast as they were made, Capital could not exist. We have, therefore, reached this certainty when we contemplate Capital; someone has worked, and has not consumed all that he has produced.

Under these circumstances, we should expect to find Capital in the hands of industrious and abstinent producers. But as Mill very justly points out: "In a rude and violent state of society it continually happens that the person who has Capital is not the very person who has saved it, but some one who, being stronger, or belonging to a more powerful community, has possessed himself of it by plunder. And even in a state of things in which property was protected, the increase of Capital has usually been, for a long time, mainly derived from privations which, though essentially the same with saving, are not generally called by that name, because not voluntary. The actual producers have been slaves, compelled to produce as much as force could extort from them, and to consume as little as the self-interest or the usually very slender humanity of their task-masters would permit." How many of our great capitalists have produced and saved until they accumulated the fortunes they possess? These fortunes are greater than any human being could save out of his makings, even if he lived most abstemiously, instead of with the luxury and ostentation of a Rothschild or a Vanderbilt. But if they have not made and saved, how came they to possess? Mill gives the answer, though he did not mean it to be applied to modern industrialism. "In a rude and violent state of society" Capital is not in the hands of the producer and saver, but in the hands of those who possess themselves "of it by plunder"—legalised plunder, in our modern days. The "saving" is not voluntary; it is "derived from privations"; the "actual producers" are wage-earners, who are "compelled to produce as much as" pressure can extort from them, and to "consume as little" in the form of wage as they can be beaten down to by the competition of the labor-market. These men "have labored, and" others "have entered into their labors".

A very brief comparison of those who produce and save, and those who possess themselves of the results of labor and abstinence, will suffice to show the inequality which characterises the present system. The worker lives hardly and dies poor, bequeathing to his children the same necessity of toil: I do not forget that the more fortunate workers have shares in Building Societies, a few pounds in the Savings Bank, and even an interest in a Burial Club, so that the parish may not have the expense of burying them; but I say that these poor successes—vast indeed in the aggregate, but paltry when the share of the individual is looked at—bear no kind of reasonable proportion to the wealth created by the worker during his life-time. On the other hand the capitalist either starts with inherited wealth, grows richer, and bequeaths the increased wealth to his children; or he begins poor, saves a little, then makes others work for him, grows rich, and bequeaths his wealth. In the second generation, the capitalist can simply invest his wealth and live on the interest; and since all interest must be paid out of the results of labor, the workers not only lose a large proportion of their produce, but this very confiscated produce is made into a future burden for them, and while the fathers build up the capitalist, the children must toil to maintain his children in idleness.

Capital may also be accumulated by the ownership of raw material, since no wealth can be produced until labor can get at this. The question of rent will be considered under the head of Land; here we are only concerned with the fact that wealth appropriated in this way is investible, and on this also interest can be obtained.

Now the enormous burden placed on labor by the investment of money at interest, is not appreciated as it ought to be. The interest on the National Debt, including terminable annuities, amounted in 1884-5 to £28,883,672 12s.; how much is paid in dividends on railway, tram-car, and companies' shares, it would be difficult to discover. Mr. Giffen, in his "Progress of the Working Classes", estimates that the capitalist classes receive from capital—excluding "wages of superintendence" and salaries—some £400,000,000 a year. In 1881, the income-tax returns quoted by Mr. Giffen show that the income from capital was no less than £407,000,000, and in estimating those in Schedules B and D (Part I.) Mr. Giffen certainly takes care to make the gains on "idle capital" as small as he can. Mr. Giffen takes the aggregate income of the whole nation at about £1,200,000,000, so that according to his own figures Capital takes more than a third part of the national income. I should be prepared to contend that the burden on the producers is heavier than he makes out, but even taking his own calculations the result is bad enough. For all this money which goes to capitalists is money *not* earned by the receivers—mark that all which is in any sense earned, as wages of superintendence, etc., is excluded—and by all this is lessened the share of the produce of labor which goes to labor.

We have already dealt with the way in which the worker suffers injustice when capital is invested in machinery owned by private individuals; we have now to consider the portion of it used as loans, cases in which the capitalist takes no part in the management of any industrial concern, but merely lends his money at usury, living on the interest he receives. There is so much confusion of thought on this subject, so much idea that a man has "a right" to invest money at interest, that it necessary to try to get at the "bed-rock" of the question. Take the case of a man who earns 30s. in a week; suppose he spends 20s. and saves 10s. For the 20s. he spends he receives their equivalent in commodities, and these he consumes; he has had his "money's worth", and he is content, and if he requires more commodities he knows he must labor again to earn their equivalent in money. The 10s. he has saved, however, are to have a different fate; they represent, also, so much possibility of possession of their equivalent in commodities which he could consume; but he desires to defer this consumption to a future day, to defer it, perhaps, until he is too old to give labor in exchange for his needs. One might suppose that the equivalent of commodities for the 10s. would be as satisfactory as the equivalent of commodities for the 20s. But it is not so. He desires to invest his 10s. at interest; let us suppose he invests it at 5 per cent.; at the end of twenty years he will have received back his 10s. by instalments of 6d. a year, and will have exchanged it for 10s. worth of commodities; yet at the end of the twenty years he expects to receive back in addition his full 10s.; to have spent it all, and yet to find it undiminished; so that for his 10s. saved he expects to receive 20s. worth of commodities in twenty years, to have his labor paid for twice over. In the case of money only is it possible to eat your cake and have it, and after you have eaten it to pass it on as large as ever to your descendants, so that they may eat it and yet find it, like the widow's cruse, ever miraculously renewed.

Those who defend usury do so generally on its supposed collateral advantages, rather than on its central theory. It is argued that "*if a man gets no interest on his savings, he has no incitement to work*". To this it may be answered: (*a*) That there is clearly no incitement to work on the part of those who live on interest, since their money comes tumbling in whether they work or idle; it is the labor of others on which the interest-receiver lives. (*b*) That the incitement to work would be greater if the reward of work were not diminished by the imposition on it of a tax for the benefit of the idle; surely the abstraction of £400,000,000 annually for interest can hardly act as an incitement to those whose labor returns are diminished to that extent. (*c*) That the real incitement to work is the desire to possess the result of labor, and that the more completely that desire is satisfied, the greater will the incitement become. Would the incitement to tramcar employees be lessened, if the necessity of paying 10 per cent on shareholder's capital no longer kept down their wages? But, in truth, this argument as to incitement to workers is either ignorant, or disingenuous. The mainspring of the worker's toil is, as a matter of fact, compulsion, not the incitement of hope of reward. Had he control over the product of his own labor, then the desire to obtain more might incite him to work harder, as indeed, has been found to be the case with piece-work, and in co-operative undertakings: with his fixed wage it is to him a matter of indifference how much or how little he produces. The desire for interest is an incitement to the capitalist to press his wage-toilers to work harder, so that after he has satisfied his own power of consumption he may lay by all the surplus value he can squeeze out of them, and increase the capital he has out at interest. The higher the interest obtainable, the greater the compulsion to work put upon the producers. But this compulsion is clearly an evil, not a good, and in the case of the tramcar employees just cited, it is compulsion which forces them to accept the long hours of labor, and the compulsion is exercised in order to obtain interest for the shareholders.

"*The incitement to thrift will disappear.*" But (*a*) the interest obtainable by "thrift" is too small to serve as an incitement, for the savings of the industrious poor are not sufficient to give interest enough to subsist on. The Savings Banks are resorted to as a convenient place wherein to put money saved for future use; it is the safe keeping of the money "for a rainy day", not the trifling interest, which is the attraction to the anxious poor. The small amount permitted to an individual and the low interest are sufficient proofs of this assertion! no one must put in more than £30 in a year, the interest is only 2¼ per cent., and this is not paid yearly, but is added to the principal. And this future necessity is the real incitement to thrift. A man earns, say, sufficient this week to support himself for a fortnight; having satisfied his needs, he does not want to satisfy them twice over; he knows that some years hence his power of work will have disappeared, while his necessity of consumption will remain, and he defers his consumption of half the results of his labor till that time. Why should he look for added power of consumption as a reward for deferring his consumption for his own convenience? Without interest, thoughtful people would save, for the sake of comfort in their old age. It may, however, be conceded that the incitement to annex the results of the thrift of others —the only way in which big fortunes can be made—will disappear with the disappearance of interest, and the possibility of living idly by taxing the labor of others.

"*It will not be possible to get money for railroads, tramcars, etc., if interest on share capital disappears.*" But the indestructible reason for making railroads, tramways, etc., is the need for the conveniences they afford. And Socialism would place the making and carrying on of all means of transit in the hands of local bodies, municipalities, and so forth, who would raise the requisite funds from the community which is to enjoy the increased facilities. These funds would be used in remuneration of the labor expended on them, and none would have a right to levy a perpetual tax on the public on the pretence of having lent the money originally employed in the construction. Now a man claims the right to tax all future labors and all future consumers for the benefit of his posterity, as a reward for having transferred into his own pockets the results of his neighbor's toil. It is time that the immorality of this claim should be pointed out, and that people should be told that while they may rightly save and live on their savings, they ought not to use their savings for the enslavement and the taxing of other people. An effective step towards the abolition of interest might be taken by the closing of the sources of idle investment, the taking over by local bodies of the local means of transit, the gas and water supply, etc., while the central authority takes over the railways.

There is, however, one argument in favor of interest which brings conviction to many minds: an individual wants to perform a piece of productive work, but has no capital and is unable to do it; he borrows the capital and performs the work; since the man who lent the capital has facilitated the doing of the work, ought he not to share in the product, which would have had no existence but for his capital? Now it might be answered to this that if his capital is returned to him in full he has lost nothing by the transaction, but has, on the contrary, gained the advantage of having his money taken care of without trouble to himself, and returned to him uninjured at the time that he requires it. But the real answer is that interest is inevitable so long as Capital remains in private hands, so long as individuals are permitted to annex the results of the unpaid labor of others, and so manufacture a lien on all future industry. Interest will only be abolished when the results of the past unpaid labor of many are held by the many to facilitate the future labor of many. Now, industry can only be carried on with the permission and the assistance of those whose stores of wealth have been piled up for them by thousands of patient toilers; and that permission and assistance can only be gained by taxing labor for the enrichment of the lender. In future those vast stores will be used to carry on production, and while labor will constantly replace the capital it uses in production, it will not also be taxed for the benefit of individuals. Interest and private property in the means of production must stand and fall together. At the present time no law against usury could be passed, and even were the passing of such a law possible it would be a dead letter, so thoroughly is the present system built on the paying of interest. All Socialists can do for the moment is to expose the fundamental dishonesty and injustice of usury, and so pave the way for a better state of things.

Apart from the abuse of Capital here indicated Capital has a function which, of course, no Socialist ignores. Capital is necessary for all forms of industry, and its function is: to save labor, as by machinery; to facilitate it, by the introduction of improvements therein; to support it while it is employed in production, and until its products are exchanged. The true use of the savings of past labor is to lighten future labor, to fertilise production. But in order that it may be thus used, it must be in the hands of the community instead of in the hands of individuals. Being as it is, and must be, the result of unpaid labor, it should pass to the community to be used for the common good, instead of to individuals to enrich them to the common loss.

Land.

Most Radicals are ready to admit that Land, *i.e.*, natural agents, ought not to be the private property of individuals. No absolute property in land is indeed recognised by the laws of this realm, but the proposition that land ought not to be private property goes, of course, much further than this legal doctrine. It declares that the soil on which a nation lives ought to belong to the nation; that those who cultivate it, or who mine in it, and who for practical purposes must have for the time the exclusive usufruct of portions of it, should pay into the national exchequer a duly-assessed sum, thus rendering an equivalent for the privilege they enjoy, and making the whole community sharers in the benefits derived from natural agents.

The present system of permitting private ownership of land has led to three great and increasing evils; the establishment of an idle class, which grows richer by increasingly taxing the industrious; the divorce of the really agricultural class from the soil; the exodus from the country districts into the towns.

Private ownership of natural agents must inevitably result in the first of these three evils. These natural agents are the basis of wealth; the very subsistence of the nation depends on their utilisation; yet a comparatively small class is permitted to claim them as private property, and to appropriate the rent to its private use. Hence, one of the first charges on the results of labor is rent, and rent, be it noted, not to the community, but to an individual who has acquired the legal right to stand between labor and land. Now just as wage is determined practically by the standard of living, so is rent determined by the same thing. The landlord exacts as rent the value of the produce minus the subsistence of the tenant, and in many cases, if the farmer's receipts sink and there is no corresponding lowering of rent, the farmer cannot even subsist, and becomes bankrupt. Hence, if a farmer improves the land and so obtains from it larger returns, the landlord steps in and raises his rent, claiming ever as his, produce minus subsistence, and confiscating for his own advantage the results of the labor and invested capital of the farmer. Thus also with the spread of commercial prosperity comes a rise in the tax levied by the landlords; as towns grow larger the land around them becomes more valuable, and thus the Stanleys grow wealthy by the growth of Liverpool, and the Grosvenors and Russells by that of London: competition drives up rents, and landlords may live in Italy or Turkey, and become ever wealthier by the growth of English trade, and the toil of English laborers. Moffat points out ("Economy of Consumpton," p. 142) that part of the retailer's profit, and possibly the larger part of it "is purely local, and which he could not carry away with him. It distinguishes the site of his business, and resolves itself into rent. If the retailer owns his own premises, he may be content with this part of his profits, and handing the business to another become a landlord. If they are owned by another, the owner, unless the retailer is able to find other suitable premises within a moderate distance, will be able to levy all the extra profit from him in the shape of rent. Hence the rapid rise of rents in the central localities of large towns." Socialists are accused of desiring to confiscate property, but the regular and uncensured confiscation of the property of busy people by idlers, the bloodsucking of the landlord leeches, passes unnoticed year by year, and Society honors the confiscators. The expropriation of small cultivators has been going on for the last 400 years, partly by big landlords buying up small ones, and partly by their thefts of common land. The story of Naboth's vineyard has been repeated in hundreds of country districts. The exorbitant rents demanded by landlords, with the pressure of American competition aided by capitalists on this side, have ruined the farming class, while the absorption of small holdings has turned into day-laborers at miserable wage the class that formerly were independent tillers of the soil. Attracted by the higher wage ruling in manufacturing towns this dislanded class has flocked into them, has crowded into unsuitable houses, increased the slums of our great cities, and, under most unwholesome condition has multiplied with terrible rapidity. The exodus has been further quickened by the letting of formerly arable land for sheep-pasture, and the consequent forced migration of the no longer needed tillers. And thus have come about the under-population of the agricultural districts, and the over-crowding of cities: too few engaged in agricultural, and too many competing for industrial, employment; until we find our own land undercultivated, and even in some districts going out of cultivation, while food is being imported to an alarming extent, and the unemployed are becoming a menace to public tranquillity. The effect on England of revolution abroad is apt to be overlooked in studying our own labor difficulties. A considerable portion of our imports represents rent and interest from estates abroad and foreign investments. This portion would suddenly stop as regards any country in which a revolution occurred, and foreign workmen were, in consequence, no longer subjected to exploitation for the benefit of English capitalists. Now this likelihood of foreign revolution is yearly increasing, and Europe is becoming more and more like a boiler with armed forces sitting on the safety valve.

The first attempt to move in the right direction was the Land Cultivation Bill introduced into the House of Commons in 1886 by Charles Bradlaugh. This proposes to expropriate landlords who hold cultivable land waste; to give them, as compensation, payment for twenty-five years equal in amount to the annual value of the produce obtained from the confiscated land—so that if there is no produce there will be no payment; to vest the land in the State, and to let it, not sell it, to cultivators. Thus, if the Bill passed, a large area of land would be nationalised early in the following year. Such an Act, followed up by others taking over all land let on building leases as they run out—probably paying to the present landlords, for life, the original ground-rents; making the Land Tax an adequate rent paid to the State; taking back without compensation all common lands that have been stolen; breaking up the big estates by crushing taxation; steps like these, if taken with sufficient rapidity, may effect a complete Land Revolution without violence, and establish Socialism so far as the ownership of natural agents is concerned.

It is of vital importance to progress in a Socialist direction that an uncomprising resistance should be offered to all schemes for the creation of new proprietors of the soil. Peasant cultivators, paying rent to the State, are good. Peasant proprietors are a mere bulwark, raised by landlords to guard their own big estates, and will delay the realisation of the true theory that the State should be the only landowner. It is also important that Socialists should popularise the idea of communal, or co-operative, farming. There can be no doubt that cereal crops can be raised most economically on large holdings, and such holdings should be rented from the body or bodies, representing the community, by groups of cultivators, so that both large and small farms should be found in agricultural districts. But it must be distinctly stated that the Socialisation of Land without the Socialisation of Capital will not solve the social problem. No replanting of the people in the soil, no improved balance of agricultural and industrial production, will by themselves free the wage-slaves of our towns. Means of production, as well as natural agents, must come under the control of the community, before the triumph of Socialism can be complete. The tendency of Radicals to aim only at the nationalisation of land has an effect, however, which will ultimately prove of service. It irritates the landlord class, and the landlords devote themselves to proving that there is no essential difference between property in Land and property in Capital. Just as they helped to pass the Factory Acts to restrain capitalists as a retort for the capitalist agitation against the Corn Laws, so they will be likely to help in nationalising Capital in revenge for the nationalisation of Land.

Education.

For the successful maintenance of a Socialist State a wide and thorough system of national education is an absolute necessity. A governed people may afford to be ignorant; a self-ruling community must be instructed, or it must perish. And the education contemplated by Socialism is a very different thing from the paltry modicum of knowledge deemed sufficient for the "masses" to-day. Under our present system education is a matter of class, and it is a misnomer to call it "national"; it is partly supported by the parents of the children who attend the Board Schools, and partly by the rates and taxes; it is limited to the mere elements of learning; the one object of the teachers is to cram the children so that they may pass stated examinations, and thus obtain a Government grant per head. Under Socialism the whole system will be revolutionised, as the one aim then will be to educate in such a way as will ensure the greatest possible healthy development of the young, with a view to their future position as members of a free community.

The foundations of complete social equality will be laid in the school. All the children will be educated in the communal schools, the only distinction being that of age. Boys and girls will not be separated as they are now, but a common education will prepare for common work. Every child will be led through a course, which will embrace a thorough training in the elements of the various sciences, so that in after life he may feel an intelligent interest in each, and if his taste so lead him, acquire later a fuller knowledge of any special branches. He—and "he" here includes "she"—will be instructed also in the elements of art, so that the sense of beauty may be developed and educated, and the refining influence of instructed taste may enrich both mind and manners. A knowledge of history, of literature, and of languages will widen sympathy and destroy narrowness and national prejudices. Nor will physical training be forgotten; gymnastics, dancing, riding, athletic games, will educate the senses and the limbs, and give vigor, quickness, dexterity, and robustness to the frame. To this will be superadded technical training, for these educated, cultured, graceful lads and lasses, are to be workers, every one of them. The foundations of this technical training will be the same for all; all will learn to cook and scrub, to dig and sew, and to render quick assistance in accidents; it is probable also that the light portions of household duties will form part of the training of every child. But as the child grows into the youth, natural capacities will suggest the special training which should be given, so as to secure for the community the full advantages which might accrue from the varied abilities of its members. No genius then will be dwarfed by early neglect, no rare ability then perish for lack of culture. Individuality will then at last find full expression, and none will need to trample on his brother in order to secure full scope for his own development. It is probable that each will learn more than a single trade—an easy task when brain acuteness and manual dexterity have been cultured—so as to promote the adaptability in the future industrial life.

Now to many, I fear to most, of my readers, this sketch of what education will be in a Socialist community will appear a mere Utopian dream. Yet is it not worth while for such to ask themselves: Why should not such an education be the natural lot of every child in a well-ordered community? Is there anything in it superfluous for the thorough development of the faculties of a human being? And if it be admitted that boys and girls thus educated would form nobler, completer, more many-sided human beings than are the men and women of to-day, is it not a rational thing to set up as an object to be worked for the realisation of an idea which would prove of incalculable benefit to the community?

It is hardly necessary to add that education in a Socialist State, would be "free"—*i.e.*, supported at the public cost, and compulsory. Free, because the education of the young is of vital importance to the community; because class distinctions can only be effaced by the training of children in common schools; because education is too important a matter to be left to the whims of individuals, and if it be removed from the parent's direction and supervision it is not just to compel him to pay for it. Compulsory, because the State cannot afford to leave its future citizens ignorant and helpless, and it is bound to protect its weak members against injustice and neglect.

Two objections are likely to be raised: the question of cost, and the question of unfitting persons for "the dirty work of the world, which someone must do".

As to cost. It must not be forgotten that this education is proposed for a Socialist community. In such a State there would be no idle adult class to be supported, but all would be workers, so that the wealth produced would be much greater than at the present time. Now according to the figures of anti-Socialist Mr. Giffen, the aggregate income of the people is at present about £1,200,000,000; of this the workers are assigned by him £620,000,000; deduct another £100,000,000 for return from investments abroad; this leaves £480,000,000 absorbed by the non-producing class. (It must be remembered, further, that a large number of the "workers" are unnecessary distributors, whose powers could be utilised to much better purpose than is done to-day.) The wealth producers have to bear the Church on their shoulders, and provide it with an income variously stated at from £6,000,000 to £10,000,000 a year. They have to bear the "landed interest", with its appropriation in rents, royalties, etc., of something like £260,000,000. They have to bear the ultimate weight of imperial and local taxation, estimated at about £120,000,000 for the present year. All these charges, by whomsoever nominally paid, have to come out of the wealth produced by the workers. Is it then to be pretended that when the idle class has disappeared there will not be wealth enough produced for the education of the children, or that their education will be as heavy a burden as the drones are to-day? Nor must it be forgotten that there are millions of acres of land that would produce wealth if labor were sent to them, and that plenty of our idlers will there find productive work which will enormously increase the national wealth. Nor also that the waste which results from luxurious idle living will be of the past, and that a simpler, manlier, rate of expenditure will have replaced the gluttony and intemperance now prevalent in the "higher circles of society".

But it will indeed be of vital importance that the proportion of workers to non-workers shall be considered, and that there shall not be in a Socialist community the over-large families which are a characteristic of the present system. Families of ten or a dozen children belong to the capitalist system, which requires for its success a numerous and struggling proletariat, propagating with extreme rapidity, so as to keep up a plentiful supply of men, women and children, for the labor market, as well as a supply of men for the army to be food for cannon, and women for the streets to be food for lust. Under a Socialist regime, the community will have something to say as to the numbers of the new members that are to be introduced into it, and for many years supported by it; and it will prefer a reasonable number of healthy, well-educated children, to a yearly huge increase which would overburden its industry. The limitation of the number in a family is a condition of Socialist success.

As to unfitting persons for work. So long as manual work is regarded as degrading, education, by increasing sensitiveness to public opinion, tends to make people shrink from it, at least if their sensitiveness is greater than their intelligence. But even now an educated person of strong will and clear judgment, who knows that all useful work is worthy of respect, finds that his education fits him to perform work more quickly and more intelligently than is possible to an ignorant person; and respecting himself in its thorough accomplishment he is conscious of no degradation. Weak persons, compelled to labor for their bread, and aware that manual work is considered to place the worker in a subordinate social class, feel ashamed of the inferior position assigned to them by public opinion; and knowing by experience that they will be snubbed if they treat their "superiors" as equals, they live down to their social rank, and long to raise their children into a class above their own. One consequence of the absurd artificial disadvantage attached to manual work, is that the children of the more successful workers crowd the inferior professional occupations, and a man prefers to be a clerk or a curate on £90 a year to being an artisan on £150. But in the Socialist State only idleness will be despised, and all useful work will be honored. There is nothing more intrinsically degrading in driving a plough than in driving a pen, although the ploughman is now relegated to the kitchen while the clerk is received in the drawing-room. The distinction is primarily a purely artificial one, but it is made real by educating the one type while the other is left ignorant, and by teaching the one to look on his work as work "fit for a gentleman", while the other is taught that his work is held in low social esteem. Each reflects the surrounding public opinion, and accepts the position assigned by it. In Socialism, both will be educated together as children; both will be taught to look on all work as equally honorable, if useful to the community; both will be cultured "gentlemen", following each his natural bent; the ploughman will be as used to his pen as the clerk; the clerk as ready to do heavy work as the ploughman; and as public opinion will regard them as equals and will hold them in equal honor, neither will feel any sense of superiority or inferiority, but they will meet on common ground as men, as members of a social unity. As to the physically unpleasant work—such as dealing with sewers, dung-heaps, etc.—much of that will probably be done by machinery, when there is no helpless class on whose shoulders it may be bound. Such as cannot be done by machinery, will probably be divided among a large number, each taking a small share thereof, and the amount done by each will thus become so insignificant, that it will be but slightly felt. In any case the profound selfishness, which would put all burden on a helot class, and rather see it brutalised by the crushing weight than bear a portion of the load on one of its fingers, must be taught that Socialism means equality, and that the divine right of idlers to live at ease on the labor of others and to be shielded by the bodies of the poor from all the unpleasantnesses of the world, is one of the notions against which Socialism wars, and which must follow the correlative superstition of the divine right of kings.

Justice.

The pretence that under the present system there is one law for rich and poor is so barefaced a piece of impudence, that it is hardly worth while to refute it. Everyone knows that a rich man is fined for an offence for which a poor man is sent to gaol; that no wise man goes to law unless he has plenty of money; that in a litigation between a rich and a poor man, the poor man practically stands no chance, for even if he at first succeeds the rich man can appeal, and, secure in the power of his money-bags, wear out his poor antagonist by costly delays and by going from court to court. The poor man cannot fee first-class counsel, seek out and bring up his witnesses from various parts of the country, and keep a stream of money continually running through his solicitor's hands. There might be the same law for him as for the rich man, if he could get it; but it is far away behind a golden gate, and he lacks the key which alone will fit the wards of the lock. Yet surely one of the primary duties of a State is to do justice among its members, and to prevent the oppression of the weak by the strong. In a civilised State justice should be dealt out without fee or reward; if a man gives up his inherent right to defend himself and to judge in his own quarrel, he ought not to be placed in a worse position than he would be in if society did not exist. Lawyers, like judges, should be officials paid by the State, and should have no pecuniary interest in winning the case in which they are engaged.

The administration of justice in a Socialist State will be a very much simpler matter than it is now. Most crimes arise from the desire to become rich, from poverty, and from ignorance. Under Socialism poverty and ignorance will have disappeared, and the desire to grow rich will have no *raison d'être* when everyone has sufficient for comfort, is free from anxiety as to his future, and sees above him no wealthy idlers whose luxury he desires to ape, and whose idleness is held up to him as a matter of envy, as the ideal state for man.

Amusement.

There is a curious inconsistency in the way in which people deal with the question of amusement at the present time. We should have an outcry about "pauperisation" and "interference with private enterprise", if anyone proposed that the theatres should be open to the public without charge. Yet Hyde Park is kept gorgeous with flowers, Rotten Row is carefully attended to, a whole staff of workers is employed, in order that the wealthy may have a fashionable and pleasant lounge; and all this is done at the national expense, without any expression of fear lest the wealthy should be pauperised by this expenditure on their behalf. Nor is complaint made of the public money spent on the other parks in London; the most that is suggested is that the money wanted ought to be taken from the London rates and not from the national taxes. No one proposes that the parks should be sold to the highest bidder, and that private enterprise should be encouraged by permitting some capitalist to buy them, and to make a charge at the gate for admission. It is significant that once anything gets under State control, the advantages are found to be so great that no one would dream of bringing it back under private exploitation. In some parks a band plays, and people are actually demoralised by listening to music for which they do not pay directly. Nay more; the British Museum, the National Gallery, the South Kensington Museum, are all open free, and no one's dignity is injured. But if the National Gallery be open free, why not the Royal Academy? If a band may be listened to in the open air without payment, why not in a concert room? And if a concert may be free, why not a theatre? Under the present system, the Royal Academy, the concert, the theatre, are all private speculations, and the public is exploited for the profit of the speculators. The National Gallery and the Museums are national property, and the nation enjoys the use of its own possessions. In a nation which has gone so far in the direction of providing intellectual amusement, it cannot be pretended that any principle is involved in the question whether or not it shall go further along the same road. A nation which collects the works of dead painters can hardly, on principle, refuse to show the works of living ones; and we Socialists may fairly urge the success of what has already been done in the way of catering for the public amusement as a reason for doing more.

As it is, with the exception of a few places, the poor, whose lives most need the light of amusement and of beauty, are relegated to the very lowest and coarsest forms of recreation. Unreal and intensely vulgar pictures of life are offered them at the theatres which specially cater for them; they never have the delight of seeing really graceful dancing, or noble acting, or of hearing exquisite music. Verily, the amusement of the wealthier leave much to be desired, and theatre and music-hall alike pander to a low and vulgar taste instead of educating and refining it; but still these are better than their analogues at the East End. Under Socialism, the theatre will become a great teacher instead of a catch-penny spectacle; and dramatists and actors alike will work for the honor of a noble art, instead of degrading their talents to catch the applause of the most numerous class of an uneducated people. Then an educated public will demand a higher art, and artists will find it worth while to study, when patient endeavor meets with public recognition, and crude impertinence suffers its due reproof. Theatres, concerts, parks, all places of public resort, will be communal property, open alike to all, and controlled by elected officers.

Conclusion.

It remains, in conclusion, to note the chief objections raised to Socialism by its opponents. Of these the most generally urged are three: that it will check individual initiative and energy; that it will destroy individuality; that it will unduly restrict personal liberty.

That it will check individual initiative and energy. This objection is founded on the idea that the impulse to initiative must always be desire for personal money gain. But this idea flies directly in the face of facts. Even under the individualistic system, no great discovery has ever been made and proclaimed merely from desire for personal money profit. The genius that invents is moved by an imperial necessity of its own nature, and wealth usually falls to the lot of the commonplace man who exploits the genius, and not to the genius itself. Even talent is moved more by joy in its own exercise, and in the public approval it wins, than by mere hope of money gain. Who would not rather be an Isaac Newton, a Shelley, or a Shakspere, than a mere Vanderbilt? And most of all are those of strong individual initiative moved by desire to serve their "larger self", which is Man. The majority of such choose the unpopular path, and by sheer strength and service gradually win over the majority. We see men and women who might have won wealth, position, power, by using their talents for personal gain in pursuits deemed honorable, cheerfully throw all aside to proclaim an unpopular truth, and to serve a cause they believe to be good and useful. And these motives will become far more powerful under Socialism than they are now. For the possession of money looms unduly large to-day in consequence of the horrible results of the want of it. The dread of hunger and of charity is the microscope which magnifies the value of wealth. But once let all men be secure of the necessaries and comforts of life, and all the finer motives of action will take their proper place. Energy will have its full scope under Socialism, and indeed when the value of a man's work is secured to him instead of the half being appropriated by someone else, it will receive a new impulse. How great will be the incentive to exertion when the discovery of some new force, or new application of a known force, means greater comfort for the discoverer *and* for all; none thrown out of work by it, none injured by it, but so much solid gain for each. It is interesting to notice, as bearing on this question, that even a partial sharing in profits by the workers stimulates invention and increases productive energy. Mr. Wordsworth Donisthorpe ("Labor Capitalisation", p. 97) quotes M. Godin as saying that the men in his "Familistère" are constantly making new inventions and improvements; and similar testimony has been borne by others who have given an interest in the business to the men they employ. In all such cases the man who invents or improves, enjoys the thanks and the praise of the community, as well as the material gain which he shares with his comrades. And let not the power of public opinion be undervalued as a stimulus to exertion. What Greek athlete would have sold his wreath of bay for its weight in gold? Only one kind of energy will be annihilated by Socialism—the energy that enslaves others for its own gain, and exploits its weaker brethren for its own profit. For this kind of energy there will be no room. The coarse purse-proud mediocrity who by sheer force of pushing brutality has trampled his way to the front, will have vanished. The man who grows rich by underpaying his employees, by being a "hard business man" will have passed away. Energy will have to find for itself paths of service instead of paths of oppression, and will be honored or reprobated according to the way in which it is used.

That it will destroy individuality. If this were true, the loss to progress would indeed be incalculable. But Socialism, instead of destroying individuality will cultivate and accentuate it, and indeed will make it possible for the first time in civilisation for the vast majority. For it needs, in order that individuality shall be developed, that the individual shall have his characteristics drawn out, and trained by education; it needs that he shall work, in maturity, at the work for which his natural abilities fit him; it needs that he shall not be exhausted by excessive toil, but shall go fresh and vigorous to his labor; it needs that he shall have leisure to continuously improve himself, to train his intellect and his taste. But such education, such choice of work, such short hours of labor, such leisure for self-culture, where are all these to-day for our laboring population? A tremendous individuality, joined to robust health, may make its way upward out of the ranks of the handworkers to-day; but all normal individuality is crushed out between the grinding-stones of the industrial mill. See the faces of the lads and lasses as they troop out of the factory, out of the great mercantile establishments; how alike they all are! They might almost have been turned out by the dozen. We Socialists demand that individuality shall be possible for all, and not only for the few who are too strong to crush.

That it will unduly restrict personal liberty. Socialism, as conceived by the non-student of it, is an iron system, in which the "State"—which is apparently separate from the citizens—shall rigidly assign to each his task, and deal out to each his subsistence. Even if this caricature were accurate, Socialism would give the great majority far more freedom than they enjoy to-day; for they would only be under the yoke for their brief hours of toil, and would have unfettered freedom, for the greater portion of their time. Contrast this compulsion with the compulsion exercised on the workers to-day by the sweater, the manager of the works or business, and above all the compulsion of hunger, that makes them bend to the yoke for the long hours of the working day, and often far into the night: and then say whether the "freedom" of Industrialism is not a heavier chain than the "tyranny" of the most bureaucratic Socialism imagined by our opponents. But the "tyranny of Socialism", however, would consist only in ordering—and enforcing the order if necessary—that every healthy adult should labor for his own subsistence. That is, it would protect the liberty of each by not allowing anyone to compel another person to work for him and by opening to all equal opportunities of working for themselves. The worker would choose his own work certainly as freely as he does now: at the present time, if one class of work has enough operatives employed at it, a man must take some other, and I do not see that Socialism could prevent this limitation of choice. At any rate, the limitation is not an argument against Socialism, since it exists at the present time.

Imagine the glorious freedom which would be the lot of each when, the task of social work complete, and done under healthy and pleasant conditions, the worker turned to science, literature, art, gymnastics, to what he would, for the joyous hours of leisure. For him all the treasures of knowledge and of beauty; for him all the delights of scenery and of art; for him all that only the wealthy enjoy to-day; all that comes from work flowing back to enrich the worker's life.

I know that our hope is said to be the dream of the enthusiast; I know that our message is derided, and that the gospel of man's redemption which we preach is scorned. Be it so. Our work shall answer the gibes of our opponents, and our faith in the future shall outlast their mockery. We know that however much man's ignorance may hinder our advance; however much his selfishness may block our path; that we shall yet win our way to the land we have seen but in our visions, and rear the temple of human happiness on the solid foundation stones of science and of truth. Above all sneer and taunt, above all laughter and bitter cries of hatred, rings out steadily our prophecy of the coming time:

"O nations undivided,
O single People, and free,
We dreamers, we derided,
We mad blind men that see,
We bear you witness ere ye come that ye shall be."

TENTH THOUSAND.]

WHY I AM A SOCIALIST.

By ANNIE BESANT.

"A Socialist! you don't mean to say you are a Socialist!" Such is the exclamation with which anyone who adopts the much-hated name of Socialist is sure to be greeted in "polite society". A Socialist is supposed to go about with his pocket full of bombs and his mind full of assassinations; he is a kind of wild beast, to be hunted down with soldiers if he lives under Bismarck, with sneers, abuse, and petty persecutions if he lives under Victoria. The very wildness of the epithets launched at him, however, shows how much there is of fear in the hatred with which he is regarded; and his opponents, by confining themselves to mere abuse, confess that they find themselves unable to cope with him intellectually. Prejudice and passion, not reasoned arguments, are the weapons relied on for his destruction. Once let the working classes understand what Socialism really is, and the present system is doomed; it is therefore of vital necessity that they shall be prevented from calmly studying its proposals, and shall be so deafened with the clamor against it that they shall be unable to hear the "still small voice" of reason. I do not challenge the effectiveness of the policy—for a time. It has been the policy of the governing classes against every movement that has been aimed against their privileges; Radicalism has been served in exactly similar fashion, and now that Radicalism has grown so strong that it can no longer be silenced by clamor, it is the turn of Socialism to pass through a like probation. There is always an ugly duckling in Society's brood; how else should be maintained the succession of swans?

With a not inconsiderable number of persons the prejudice against the name of Socialist is held to be a valid reason for not adopting it, and it is thought wiser to advocate the *thing* without affronting the antagonism aroused against the *name.* With such a policy I have ever had no sympathy. It seems to me the wiser, as well as the franker course, to boldly wear any name which expresses an opinion held, and live down the prejudice it may awaken. The name Socialist is in itself a fine name, connoting as it does the social union; it is the recognised label of the school which holds as its central doctrine that land and the means of production should be the property of the social union, and not of privileged individuals in it; it is the one name which is recognised all the world over as the name of those who are opposed to political, religious, and social tyranny in every land; of those who look with brotherly sympathy on the efforts of every nation which is struggling for its freedom; of those who are on the side of the poor and the toiling everywhere; of those who recognise no barriers of nationality, of class, or of creed, but who see a brother in every worker, a friend in every lover of the people. Every political name is of the country in which it is born; but the name Socialist, like the name Atheist, is of no one land; it is valid in every country; it is whispered on Russian steppe, in German field, in French city, in Italian vineyard; and wherever it is heard the chains of the captive for a moment seem lighter, for Hope has lifted them, and the careworn faces of the toilers brighten, as a gleam from a sunnier day gilds the tools over which they bow.

Pass we from the name to the thing, from "the outer and visible sign to the inward and spiritual grace". Within the compass of a brief paper it is not possible for me to give all the reasons which have made me a Socialist, but there are three main lines of thought along which I travelled towards Socialism, and along which I would fain persuade my readers to travel also, in the hope that they too may find that they lead to the same goal.

I. *I am a Socialist because I am a believer in Evolution.* The great truths that organisms are not isolated creations, but that they are all linked together as parts of one great tree of life; that the simple precedes the complex; that progress is a process of continued integrations, and ever-increasing differentiations; these truths applied to the physical animated world by Darwin, Huxley, Haeckel, Büchner, and their followers, have unravelled the tangles of existence, have illuminated the hidden recesses of Nature. But the service to be done to science by Evolution was not completed when natural history was made a coherent whole instead of a heterogeneous heap of irrelevant facts; its light next fell on the universe of mind, and traced the growth of mentality from the lowest organism that responds to a stimulus up to the creative brain of man. And still it had work to do, and next it reduced to order the jarring elements of the sphere of morals, and analysed duty and conscience, right and wrong, obligation and responsibity, until it rendered intelligible and consequent all that seemed supernatural and incoherent. And both in mind and in morals Spencer was the great servant of Evolution, illuminating the previous darkness by lucid exposition and by pregnant suggestion. But having done so much in the ordering of thought in every realm of study save one, it was not possible that Evolution should leave Sociology untouched, a mere chaos of unrelated facts, of warring opinions. Hither also came the light, and out of the chaos slowly grew a cosmos. Society was seen evolving from lowliest savagery, from the embryonic state of barbarism, through nomad life to settled order, through tribes to nation, through feudalism to industrialism, through industrialism to —— Nowhither? Evolution complete? Further progress barred? Not so. For science, which cannot prophesy details of the future, can grasp tendencies of the present, and recognising the conditions of the social growth of the past, can see how the present has been moulded, and along which lines its further development must inevitably pass. Now the progress of society has been from individualistic anarchy to associated order; from universal unrestricted competition to competition regulated and restrained by law, and even to partial co-operation in lieu thereof. Production from being individualistic has become cooperative; large bodies of workmen toiling together have replaced the small groups of masters and apprentices; factory production has pushed aside cottage production, and industrial armies are seen instead of industrial units. Laws for the regulation of industry—which failed when they were made by a few for their own advantage, and were used in the vain effort to keep down the majority—have been carried and applied successfully to some extent in defence of the liberty of the majority against the oppression of a privileged few. Since the partial admission of the workers to the exercise of political power, these laws for the regulation of industry have rapidly multiplied, and at the same time laws which hindered the free association of the workers have been repealed. The State has interfered with factories and workshops, to fix the hours of labor, to insist on sanitary arrangements, to control the employment of the young. Land Acts and Ground Game Acts, Education Acts and Shipping Acts, Employers' Liability Acts and Artisans' Dwellings Acts, crowd our Statute book. Everywhere the old ideas of free contract, of non-interference, are being outraged by modern legislation. And it is not only Socialists who point to these reiterated interferences as signs of the tendencies of society. John Morley, in his "Life of Cobden", notes that England, where Socialism is supposed to have but small influence, has a body of Socialistic legislation greater than can found in any other country in the world.

II. *I am a Socialist because of the failure of our present civilisation.* In an article which appeared in the July number of the *Westminster Review*, after alluding to Professor Huxley's declaration that he would rather have been born a savage in one of the Fiji islands than have been born in a London slum, I put the following question, which I will venture to quote here. "Is it rational that the progress of society should be as lopsided as it is? Is it necessary that, while civilisation brings to some art, beauty, refinement—all that makes life fair and gracious—it should bring to others drudgery, misery, degradation, such as no uncivilised people know? and these emphasised and rendered the bitterer by the contrast of what life is to many, the dream of what it might be to all. For Professor Huxley is right. The savage has the forest and the open sea, the joy of physical strength, food easily won, leisure sweet after the excitement of the chase; the civilised toiler has the monotonous drudgery of the stuffy workshop, the hell of the gin-palace for his pleasure-ground, the pandemonium of reeking court and stifling alley for his lullaby; civilisation has robbed him of all natural beauty and physical joy, and has given him in exchange—the slum. It is little wonder that, under these circumstances, there are many who have but scant respect for our social fabric, and who are apt to think that any change cannot land them in a condition worse than that in which they already find themselves."

Now if this view should spread widely among the inhabitants of the slums, it is obvious that the present civilisation would stand in very considerable peril, and it would be likely to sink, as feudalism sank in France, beneath the waves of a popular revolution. But such a revolution, sweeping from the slums over the happier parts of the towns, would not be a revolution set going by men of genius, directed by men of experience and of knowledge, as was the French Revolution of 1789. It would be a mad outburst of misery, of starvation, of recklessness, which would for a brief space sweep everything before it, and behind it would leave a desolate wilderness. Walk at midnight through the streets near the Tower, along Shadwell High Street, or about "Tiger Bay", and imagine what would happen if those drunken men and women, singing, shouting, fighting, in the streets, were to burst the barriers that hem them in, and were to surge westwards over London, wrecking the civilisation which had left them to putrefy in their misery, and had remained callous to their degradation. Is it not the part of a good citizen to try to change a social system which bears such products as these in every great city?

The slum population, however, is not wholly composed of such persons as I have spoken of. Large numbers of honest, temperate, industrious people are forced by poverty, and by the necessity of being near their work, into the dismal fate of living in the slums. And among them is spreading a discontent which is pregnant with change. Education is awakening in them desires and hopes which find no satisfaction in the slums. It is opening to them wider views of human life, and the penny newspaper tells them of enjoyments and luxuries of which they would have known nothing, pent in the dreary mill-round of their toiling lives, had ignorance kept them blind. Slowly is being formed that "educated proletariat" which shall work out its own salvation, and which shall refuse any longer to act as the basis on which is reared the pyramid of civilisation. The present civilisation rests on the degradation of the workers; in order that they may accept their lot they must be kept poor, ignorant, submissive; the culture of their superiors is paid for with their ignorance; the graceful leisure of the aristocrat is purchased by the rough toil of the plebeian; his dainty fingers are kept soft and white by the hardening and reddening of the poor man's hands; the workers are daily sacrificed that the idlers may enjoy. Such is modern civilisation. Brilliant and beautiful where it rises into the sunlight, its foundation is of human lives made rotten with suffering. Whited sepulchre in very truth, with its outer coating of princes and lords, of bankers and squires, and within filled with dead men's bones, the bones of the poor who builded it.

Most hopeful sign, perhaps, for the future is the fact that discontent with the present system is not confined to those who are in a special sense its victims. In every class of society are found men and women who look and work for a complete revolution in the method of the production and distribution of wealth. Among those who profit most by the present system are found the most eager workers against it, and many whose lot is cast among the "comfortable classes" are striving to undermine the very constitution which gives them the privileges they enjoy. In them sympathy has triumphed over selfishness, and their own rich wine of life tastes sour when they see the bitter water of poverty pressed to their brothers' lips. They are indignant that their own hands should be so full while others' hands are empty; and would fain lessen their own heap in order that the share of their neighbors may be made equal with their own.

At present the Socialist movement in England is far more a middle-class than a working-class one; the creed of Socialism is held as an intellectual conviction by the thoughtful and the studious, and is preached by them to the workers, who have everything to gain by accepting it, and some of whom have already embraced and are teaching it. Instead of being a class movement, it is a movement of men and women of all classes for a common end, and the Socialist army is composed of persons of various social ranks, who have renounced for themselves the class distinctions they are banded together to destroy.

III. *I am a Socialist because the poverty of the workers is, and must continue to be, an integral part of the present method of wealth-production and wealth-distribution.* Under that method land, capital, and labor, the three factors in wealth-production, are divorced from each other, and landless, capitalless labor—which must sell itself to live—lies at the mercy of the privileged classes. The owner of the land demands a share of the produce raised on or from it, and this share is claimed by him not because he helps in gaining the produce, but because he owns the raw material of the soil, and can prevent anyone from utilising it, if he so pleases. The land is his; for him the rain softens and the sunshine warms the soil; for him sweet Mother Nature bares her fragrant bosom, and pours out the treasures with which her arms are laden; for him she has been working through the silent centuries, growing her forests, carbonising her buried vegetable treasures, storing her vast unseen realms with gem and ore of metal, building through myriads of ages by life and death, by creation and destruction, by swift birth and slow decay. And all this toil of ages, wrought out by the mighty unseen forces, finds its end in my Lord Emptyhead, who stretches out his useless hands over the noble product, and cries to his countless brothers, "This is mine!". Then he bargains with them, and claims the right to tax their labor in exchange for permitting them to use what ought to be the common property, and to tax it, moreover, in proportion to its success. Thus Dukes of Westminster, of Bedford, and of Portland; Marquises of Londonderry, of Anglesey, and of Bute; Earls of Derby and of Dudley; with many another beside; all these grow ever and ever wealthier, not because they work, but because their ancestors by force or fraud got grip of the soil, and in days when the people were unrepresented made laws which secured to them and their descendants the monstrous monopoly of natural agents. As the people multiply and press ever more and more on the means of subsistence, they have to pay more and more to the owners thereof; and while private property in land is permitted to exist, so long will the landless lie at the landlord's mercy, and wealthy idler and poverty-stricken worker will form integral parts of our social, or rather anti-social, system.

Similarly is a share of the worker's product claimed by the class which holds as individual property the accumulated wealth made by generations of toilers, the present means of production; this wealth is obtained by forcing labor to accept as "wage" less than the value it creates; unless it will accept these terms it is not permitted to create any value at all, so that it has the choice between starvation and exploitation. The share of its own produce which it receives as wage varies from time to time; sometimes it is less, sometimes more; but it is always less than the value made by it. Only when there is a "profit" to be made—that is when the capitalist can get out of his "hands" more value than he returns to them as wage—will he employ them. The machines which have been invented by human genius, and which ought to lessen human labor, are used to make fortunes for a few. A skilful workman sees a possible improvement; his master reaps the profit of the improved machine, patenting it for his own enrichment. Huge fortunes rapidly made date from the invention of machinery, because only by the possession of machinery can a man utilise the labor of many for such swift gain. Possessing this, he is in a position of advantage which enables him to say to his fellow-men: "You shall use my machinery on condition that you are content with bare subsistence, and leave to me the wealth which flows from you and the machine". Thus machinery, which is one of the advantages of civilisation, gives wealth to its individual owner, and bare subsistence to the toilers who work with it. And so long as the possession of all the mechanical advantages is in the hands of individuals, so long will they be able to enslave and exploit those who have only their natural tools, and the machine-owner may lie at his ease and watch the growing piles of his wealth, as his bondmen heap it together, and gratefully accept the fraction of it which his higher servants fling to them as wage. Poverty will last so long as one class depends on another for "employment"; so long as one man must sell another man his labor at whatever rate the condition of the market may fix. Free men may associate their labor for a common end, and divide the common product; slaves are obliged to let their labor be at the direction of their master, and to accept subsistence in exchange.

Class distinctions will endure while men stand in the position of employer and employed; the one who holds the means of subsistence feels himself superior to the one who craves them. And this is not all. The life-surroundings of the rich fashion an organism easily distinguishable from the organism produced by the life-surroundings of the poor. Take two healthy week-old babies, one the child of a ploughman and the other the child of a duke; place them side by side, and the keenest eye will not be able to separate the aristocrat and the plebeian. But give to one the best education and to the other none, and place them side by side when each is grown to manhood, and the easy polished manner and soft speech of the one will be contrasted with the clumsy roughness and stumbling articulation of the other. Education, training, culture, these make class distinctinctions, and nothing can efface them save common education and equally refined life-surroundings. Such education and life-surroundings cannot be shared so long as some enjoy wealth they do not earn, and others are deprived of the wealth they do earn. Land and capital must be made common property, and then no man will be in a position to enslave his brother by placing before him the alternative of starvation or servitude. And because no system save that of Socialism claims that there shall be no individual monopoly of that on which the whole nation must depend, of the soil on which it is born and must subsist, of the capital accumulated by the labor of its innumerable children, living and dead; because no system save that of Socialism claims for the whole community control of its land and its capital; because no system save that of Socialism declares that wealth created by associated workers should be shared among those workers, and that no idlers should have a lien upon it; because no system save that of Socialism makes industry really free and the worker really independent, by substituting co-operation among workers for employed and employing classes; because of all this I am a Socialist. My Socialism is based on the recognition of economic facts, on the study of the results which flow inevitably from the present economic system. The pauper and the millionaire are alike its legitimate children; the evil tree brings forth its evil fruits.

PRICE ONE PENNY.

Printed by ANNIE BESANT and CHARLES BRADLAUGH, at 63, Fleet Street, London, E.C.—1886.

RADICALISM AND SOCIALISM.

BY

ANNIE BESANT.

[Reprinted from "Our Corner".]

LONDON:
FREETHOUGHT PUBLISHING COMPANY,
63, FLEET STREET, E.C.
1887.

PRICE THREEPENCE.

RADICALISM AND SOCIALISM.

Among the various features of public life in England at the present time there is none which appears to me to be more regrettable, or more fruitful of evil consequences in the near future, than the antagonism between Radicalism and Socialism—or rather between Radicals and Socialists—which is so strongly marked on the platform and in the press. As a Socialist, it is with much regret that I am forced to acknowledge that the first provocation came from the Socialist side, and that it was the uncalled-for and unscrupulous abuse poured out on Radical leaders and workers which stirred up the anger of the Radicals, and caused reprisals as bitter as the attacks. The taunts and sneers levelled at working men's Radical organisations; the description of some of their most active and trusted officials as "fifth-rate political hacks"; the insolent contempt expressed by bran-new "leaders" for men who had been toiling for the popular cause for more years of service than they could themselves count months; all these things alienated the more self-reliant and thoughtful of the workers, and made them look with coldness, deeply tinged with dislike, on any idea which was presented to them under the guise of Socialism. The whole mischief has been done by a very small and very narrow-minded clique, the members of which have nothing but abuse for everyone who does not meekly follow in their wake, and who appear to be moved by a furious jealousy against everyone, Socialist or non-Socialist, who is able to serve the cause of the workers, and is regarded by them with trust and with love. It is time that it should be clearly seen that these few Socialists who are constantly attacking Radicals speak only for themselves, and not for English Socialists in general, but that, on the contrary, most of the latter desire earnestly to work with their Radical brethren for all objects which both parties regard as desirable; and that while they hold up steadily as their object the complete Socialisation of the State, they will gladly welcome the companionship of the Radicals over that portion of the road which the Radicals are ready to travel. No worse mischief can be done to the cause of labor, no more serious harm can be done to progress, than by setting Radicals and Socialists in antagonism, instead of binding them together; than by putting in opposite camps those who ought to be banded against the common foe; than by using wild and bitter words to drive apart those whose earnest desire is for the common good, and so, by dividing the army of progress, to render it easier for the privileged classes to defend their citadel of idleness and monopoly. The position that I desire to advance is that Socialism is the outcome, the legitimate and necessary outcome, of Radicalism; that the main current of Radical legislation, despite little eddies and backwaters, sets towards Socialism; and that just as Evolution, taking up the chaos of biological facts, set them forth as an intelligible and correlated order, so Socialism, dealing with the chaos of sociological facts, brings a unifying principle, which turns Radicalism from a mere empirical system into a reasoned, coherent, and scientific whole. Socialism is a far vaster thing than a changed system for the production and distribution of wealth, great as that economical change would be; it means the substitution, as method, of co-operation for competition in every department of human life; it means the substitution, as aim, of the common good for the personal profit of the individual; it means the placing of the production and distribution of wealth, as well as of all public affairs in which men and women are associated, under the control of bodies elected by and responsible to those who are concerned in them, whether as workers or as citizens, instead of leaving them, as so many of them now are, under individual authority.

Now it is impossible to realise what Socialism means, and to study the history of our own times with intelligence and insight, without recognising the vast revolution which has been going on during the present century, and without seeing that the changes which are being wrought are on the road of which Socialism is the natural and inevitable end. Radical legislation in removing privilege, in placing public affairs in the hands of the populace, in assailing landlord monopoly, in regulating the relations between employer and employed, is penetrated by the Socialist spirit, and has already leavened the community with Socialist ideas. At the beginning of the century there was little Socialism in our legislation; there was no interference on the part of the State between employers and employed, save in the way of tying down the employed and of preventing them from associating together for their common good. Of restrictions on the workers for the benefit of the exploiting classes there had been enough and to spare; but of legislation to equalise conditions, to check the strong in his oppression of the weak, to utilise the powers arising from the social union for the common benefit, of this there had been nothing. All that the commercial classes asked for was to be left alone by the State; they were willing to destroy laws which favored the landlord interest—as the Corn Laws—but they demanded for themselves merely a free hand; strong in their position of advantage, holding in their hands the means of subsistence of the population which seethed below them, they only required to be left "free" in order to gain their ends; free, that was, to use starvation as a whip with which to coerce the workers if they turned restive under their burdens, to buy them in the labor-market as "hands" to drive their machines, to pile up the riches made by the toiling myriads, flinging back to them as "wage" a fraction of the wealth they created. There were then no laws to regulate the conditions of labor; any man, who had the power to do so, might build up a fortune by the overwork of men, women, and children. At that time the democracy had no share in the Government; the workers were voiceless in the great Council of England, and were therefore wholly at the mercy of their employers. It was not until the degradation of the working population, the absolute physical ruin of hundreds and of thousands of the people, had become so patent that it could no longer be denied, that the State stepped in between the employer and the children he was murdering by over-work, and limited the hours during which, and the conditions under which, the children should be permitted to labor. Since that first interference with so-called "freedom of contract" there have been many others, some of which touched the "Rights of Property"; such as the Factory Acts which limited the hours of labor, and insisted on proper sanitary conditions, the Shipping, Irish Land, Agricultural Holdings, Employer's Liability, and Education Acts—all cases in which the State interfered with individual "rights" for the sake of effecting the common good. Thick-and-thin opponents of Socialism have been quick to notice this Socialist tendency of legislation, since the working classes have been able to influence Parliament. The Liberty and Property Defence League remarks that "every fresh curtailment of individual liberty, or substitution of collective for individual action in the assumed interest of the community, is a step in the direction of State Socialism", and it issues from time to time a list of the proposed measures which tend in this direction. Lord Pembroke complains that "Land Acts, Shipping Acts, Education Acts, Factory and Workshops Acts, Water Company Acts, and all the rest of them", are regarded "as exceptions that are justified by the circumstances of the particular case" by people who are not Socialists, whereas "each one that is added to the list weakens popular belief in the principles of freedom, and inclines it towards those of Socialism". Lord Wemyss, in a speech delivered in the House of Lords on July 31st, 1885, enumerated seven Acts and eight Bills between 1870 and 1885 that assumed "the right of the State to regulate the management of or to confiscate real property—steps in the direction of substituting 'land nationalisation' for individual ownership"; there were four Bills affecting corporate bodies in 1885, two of which dealt with Water Companies, and were "attempts to subject the chartered rights of private enterprise in water supply to municipal monopolies, by first reducing the value of the companies' property by harassing legislation"; then nine Acts affecting ships, and six affecting mines, which regulated "private enterprise and individual management"; nine Acts and three Bills regulating manufactures and trades, and six Railway Acts, "encroachments by the Board of Trade upon the self-government of private enterprise in railways". Passing over twenty Acts and six Bills about the Liquor Traffic, we come to sixteen Acts and three Bills which "embody the principle that it is the duty of the State to provide dwellings, private gardens, and other conveniences for the working classes, and assume its right to appropriate land for these purposes". Then thirteen Acts and four Bills on Education and Recreation, many of which "provide those things that ought to be left to the instincts and affections of the parents". "While on the Continent", said Lord Wemyss, "people are thinking and vaporing about Socialism, we in this country are adopting it in our legislation. Louise Michel, the French Communist, epitomised the matter very effectively when she said 'that whereas in France Socialists stand in the dock, in England they sit in the House of Commons'." Herbert Spencer in his "Man *versus* the State" summarises the legislation of the last twenty-five years, in order to show the increase of State interference which has taken place "during periods of Liberal ascendancy". Despite its length, I quote it here, so important is the testimony borne in it to the soundness of my position :

"To bring the illustrations within compass, let us commence with 1860, under the second administration of Lord Palmerston. In that year the restrictions of the Factories Act were extended to bleaching and dyeing works; authority was given to provide analysts of food and drink, to be paid out of local rates; there was an Act providing for inspection of gasworks, as well as for fixing quality of gas and limiting price; there was the Act which, in addition to further mine inspection, made it penal to employ boys under twelve not attending school, and unable to read and write. In 1861 occurred an extension of the compulsory provisions of the Factories Act to lace-works; power was given to poor-law guardians, etc., to enforce vaccination; local boards were authorised to fix rates of hire—horses, ponies, mules, asses, and boats—and certain locally-formed bodies had given to them powers of taxing the locality for rural drainage and irrigation works, and for supplying water to cattle. In 1862 an Act was passed for restricting the employment of women and children in open-air bleaching; and an Act for making illegal a coal-mine with a single shaft, or with shafts separated by less than a specified space, as well as an Act giving the Council of Medical Education the exclusive right to publish a Pharmacopœia, the price of which is to be fixed by the Treasury. In 1863 came the extension of compulsory vaccination to Scotland, and also to Ireland; there came the empowering of certain boards to borrow money repayable from the local rates, to employ and pay those out of work; there came the authorising of town authorities to take possession of neglected ornamental spaces, and rate the inhabitants for their support; there came the Bakehouses Regulation Act, which, besides specifying minimum age of employees occupied between certain hours, prescribed periodical lime-washing, three coats of paint when painted, and cleaning with hot water and soap at least once in six months; and there came also an Act giving a magistrate authority to decide on the wholesomeness or unwholesomeness of food brought before him by an inspector. Of compulsory legislation dating from 1864, may be named an extension of the Factories Act to various additional trades, including regulations for cleansing and ventilation, and specifying of certain employees in match-works, that they might not take meals on the premises, except in the wood-cutting places. Also, there were passed a Chimney-Sweepers Act; an Act for further regulating the sale of beer in Ireland; an Act for compulsory testing of cables and anchors; an Act extending the Public Works Act of 1863, and the Contagious Diseases Act, which last gave the police, in specified places, powers which, in respect of certain classes of women, abolished sundry of those safeguards to individual freedom established in past times. The year 1865 witnessed further provision for the reception and temporary relief of wanderers at the cost of ratepayers; another public-house closing Act; and an Act making compulsory regulations for extinguishing fires in London. Then, under the ministry of Lord John Russell in 1866, have to be named an Act to regulate cattle-sheds, etc., in Scotland, giving local authorities powers to inspect sanitary conditions, and fix the numbers of cattle; an Act forcing hop-growers to label their bags with the year and place of growth, and the true weight, and giving police powers of search; an Act to facilitate the building of lodging-houses in Ireland, and providing for regulation of the inmates; a Public Health Act, under which there is registration of lodging-houses and limitation of occupants, with inspection and directions for lime-washing, etc., and a Public Libraries Act, giving local powers by which a majority can tax a minority for their books.

"Passing now to the legislation under the first ministry of Mr. Gladstone, we have, in 1869, the establishment of State telegraphy with the accompanying interdict on telegraphing through any other agency; we have the empowering a Secretary of State to regulate hired conveyances in London; we have further and more stringent regulations to prevent cattle diseases from spreading, another Beer-house Regulation Act, and a Sea Birds Preservation Act (ensuring greater mortality of fish). In 1870 we had a law authorising the Board of Public Works to make advances for landlords' improvements and for purchase by tenants; we have the Act, which enables the Education

Department to form school boards which shall purchase sites for schools, and may provide free schools supported by local rates, and enabling school-boards to pay a child's fees; to compel parents to send their children, etc., etc.; we have a further Factories and Workshops Act, making, among other restrictions, some on the employment of women and children in fruit-preserving and fish-curing works. In 1871 we meet with an amended Merchant Shipping Act, directing officers of the Board of Trade to record the draught of sea-going vessels leaving port; there is another Factory and Workshops Act, making further restrictions; there is a Pedlar's Act, inflicting penalties for hawking without a certificate, and limiting the district within which the certificate holds, as well as giving the police power to search pedlars' packs; and there are further measures for enforcing vaccination. The year 1872 had, among other Acts, one which makes it illegal to take for hire more than one child to nurse, unless in a house registered by the authorities, who prescribe the number of infants to be received; it had a Licensing Act, interdicting sale of spirits to those apparently under sixteen; and it had another Merchant Shipping Act, establishing an annual survey of passenger steamers. Then, in 1873, was passed by the Agricultural Children's Act, which makes it penal for a farmer to employ a child who has neither certificate of elementary education nor of certain prescribed school-attendances, and there was passed a Merchant Shipping Act, requiring on each vessel a scale showing draught, and giving the Board of Trade power to fix the numbers of boats and life-saving appliances to be carried out.

"Turn now to Liberal law-making under the present Ministry. We have, in 1880, a law which forbids conditional advance-notes in payment of sailors' wages; also a law which dictates certain arrangements for the safe carriage of grain cargoes; also a law increasing local coercion over parents to send their children to school. In 1881 comes legislation to prevent trawling over clam-beds and bait-beds, and an interdict making it impossible to buy a glass of beer on Sunday in Wales. In 1882 the Board of Trade was authorised to grant licenses to generate and sell electricity; and municipal bodies were enabled to levy rates for electric-lighting; further, exactions from rate-payers were authorised for facilitating more accessible baths and washhouses, and local authorities were empowered to make bye-laws for securing the decent lodging of persons engaged in picking fruit and vegetables. Of such legislation during 1883 may be named the Cheap Trains Act, which, partly by taxing the nation to the extent of £100,000 a year (in the shape of relinquished passenger duty), and partly at the cost of railway proprietors, still further cheapens travelling for workmen; the Board of Trade, through the Railway Commissioners, being empowered to ensure sufficiently good and frequent accommodation. Again, there is the Act which, under penalty of £10 for disobedience, forbids the payment of wages to workmen at or within public-houses; there is another Factory and Workshop Act, commanding inspection of white-lead works (to see that they are provided with overalls, respirators, baths, acidulated drinks, etc.) and of bakehouses, regulating times of employment of both, and prescribing in detail some constructions for the last, which are to be kept in a condition satisfactory to the inspectors" (pp. 9–12).

After carefully following out the results of this policy, Herbert Spencer asks whither these changes "with the accompanying current of ideas" are carrying us, and he finally answers: "Thus influences of various kinds conspire to increase corporate action and decrease individual action. And the change is being on all sides aided by schemers, each of whom thinks only of his pet project, and not at all of the general reorganisation which his, joined with others such, are working out. It is said that the French Revolution devoured its own children. Here an analogous catastrophe seems not unlikely. The numerous Socialistic changes made by Act of Parliament, joined with the numerous others presently to be made, will by-and-bye be merged in State Socialism—swallowed in the vast wave which they have little by little raised" (pp. 26, 33, 34).

Now in all these separate steps towards Socialism, Radicals have advocated the particular measure on the ground of its individual usefulness, but they have not grasped the underlying tendency of the whole body of allied changes. The main difference between Radicals and Socialists in dealing with these practical questions is that Radicals take the steps towards Socialism without recognising whither they are going; while the Socialists see the goal as well as the steps, and recognise the general tendency of legislation as well as the separate Acts of Parliament. They have risen from empiricism to science. But in this difference lies no reason for quarrel, no cause for antagonism. There is, however, a cause of disagreement that might well arise between Radicals and Socialists as politicians, due to the fact that Socialists scrutinise the tendency of legislation as well as its immediate results. For instance peasant proprietorship, as distinguished from peasant tenancy, of land has many advocates among Radicals; to any legislation in this direction Socialists would offer au uncompromising resistance, as being retrograde in tendency, and as increasing the difficulty of bringing all land under the control of the community. But such disagreement on an isolated measure would not prevent full and cordial co-operation in matters on which both partics were agreed. And in order to dispose Radicals to such co-operation I point them to the legislation of our own generation, and I challenge them to disprove the assertion that this body of legislation tends to substitute collective control for individual independence, to limit private rights of property, to interfere in the name of the community between employer and employed, between parent and child, and to take over important branches of national enterprise into the hands of the State.

It is not only in legislation that the spirit of Socialism is making itself felt, but we see it again in the growing inclination of municipalities to extend the sphere of their activity, and to undertake the supply of important necessaries of life over the district they are elected to administer. The substitution of Socialism for individualism in matters affecting the citizens of any locality, is the substitution of the action of an elected body for private enterprise in supplying the wants of the community, and the consequent regarding of all excess of receipts over expenditure as being funds belonging to the community, and not to the individuals who have superintended the business out of which they may have arisen. I may take as a convenient illustration of the change from individualism to Socialism in the supply of one necessary of life, the methods in which a community may obtain its water. Each might buy as much water as he wanted from a private trader at a charge fixed by competition; or he might sink a well in his own back garden, and if he were very energetic and enterprising he might sink it deeper than the wells of his neighbors, and so obtain more water than he wanted for his own use, while their wells ran dry; in either of these cases, the water-supply of the town would be left to individual enterprise. Another individualistic method would consist in a body of men voluntarily associating themselves into a company for the supply of water; such a company would obtain an Act of Parliament giving it certain rights and privileges, and would levy a water-rate on the inhabitants of the district it supplied; the profits made would be pocketed by the company, and divided among the shareholders. But the water supply might be undertaken by the municipality elected by the community; the rate would then be fixed at a figure estimated to cover the cost, and if any profit should arise the profit would go into the town exchequer, and would be used for the benefit of the community. This would be Socialism, applied to the supply of water. Some few towns have already taken this step, and have found as result that the water-supply is better and cheaper when controlled by the municipality than when managed for the individuals. The supply of gas, again, is being undertaken by municipalities with very satisfactory results. In some cases gas is supplied at a cheaper rate than when it was in the hands of a private company, and at the same time there has been an excess of receipts over expenditure which has gone to the lessening of the rates. So blind are many to the real character of the changes taking place before their eyes, that while they would denounce the supply of milk or bread by the municipality as sheer Socialism, they regard with approval the supply by it of gas and water. Really each such step, placing the distribution of a necessary of life in the hands of an elected body, which trades in it for the advantage of a community electing it, is a step towards Socialism, and this growth of municipal Socialism, fostered and encouraged by the Radicals, shows how far unconscious Socialism has spread. It has already been proposed that the liquor trade shall be undertaken by the municipality, and Mr. Chamberlain has been a warm advocate of this (the Gothenburg) scheme. It is not so very far from this to the establishment of municipal stores, stores that would soon become popular from the purity of their goods and the lowness of their prices.

Now this growth of municipal Socialism, visible on all hands, cannot continue without a corresponding growth over a wider area, the area of the State. Already in the Post Office there is the beginning of the Socialism of the State; here the State has taken upon itself the functions of collecting and distributing the letters of the whole community; similarly it has taken in hand the business of telegraphing, and is taking that of conveying parcels; the superior certainty and celerity of the State carriage of parcels are being widely recognised, and the business is rapidly growing. Who now hesitates, if he wants to send a small parcel from London to Dundee, between the means of conveyance directed by the State, and those controlled by "private enterprise"? Nor is it, as has been suggested, any argument against the Socialist character of the Post Office that the charge made varies with the weight carried; Socialism estimates the value of a thing by the amount of human labor required to produce it, and those who require the expenditure of more human labor for their service must in exchange give more of their own labor, that is, of the results thereof. Socialism implies the equal exchange of equal amounts of labor, and only forbids that a third party who adds nothing should make a profit out of the exchange. It does not mean the distribution of everything in equal proportions, without any regard to what each one does. Nor is it necessary to Socialism that all the details of a business concern with many branches should be arranged from a single State centre. The Post Office, which is a State institution, is not governed in its minute details from St. Martin's-le-Grand. From the centre come certain laws and regulations which all must observe; but it is not the State which chooses the country postmen; it is not the State which controls the minutiæ of the work of the individual letter-carrier. He takes his order from the postmaster of his district, and not from the Postmaster-General. And so, in all kinds of business, under Socialism, there will be group after group, co-ordinate with each other, each being related to the wider group next above it; and the individual laborer would come into contact with his own group, not with the central executive. But we can see in the Post Office organisation the enormous gain of a central unifying power. When a great political speech is to be delivered, to telegraph which over the country would utterly overtax a local staff, then the central body steps in to supply the sudden demand, and affords the help necessary for the due discharge of the public service. While industry is under individual control, we have industrial anarchy; in one place there are too many workers, in another too few, and equilibrium is only attained after much friction and much suffering, to be again overthrown by the next fluctuation. But with a central regulative body, supply may be made to meet demand, and what is now done by the Post Office in a single branch would be done in all departments of industry. Then labor would be organised without waste and without excess, and while laborers would be as free as Post Office clerks are now, all profits made would come back to the nation as a whole; so that instead of individualistic gain there would be corporate good and corporate advantage everywhere. Radicals recognise the utility of the State collection and distribution of one kind of article—letters. Is there any difference *in principle* between the State collecting the letters of a district and collecting the goods manufactured in it? between distributing the letters and distributing the goods? In the latter case it would not need to do as much as it does with the letters; it delivers them at individual houses; it would only need to deliver the goods at district stores. Under such conditions, there would be no more fruit rotting in Yorkshire because its sale would not pay the cost of carriage, while high prices were being paid for similar fruit in London; no more exorbitant railway charges and middleman's profits eating up the whole price paid by the consumer.

Radicals, again, are to a great extent in favor of placing all the means of communication under State control. Many Radicals demand that all tramcars, omnibuses, and hackney carriages plying in a town shall be transferred to the municipality of the town, and that the railways shall be acquired by the State. Here once more Radicals desire that representative bodies shall acquire property and administer it for the general advantage; that any gains accruing shall go into the general exchequer; that public good, not private gain, shall be sought. But every step which substitutes agents of the community for men working for individual gain is a step towards Socialism; and when Radicals have taken all the steps the Socialist State will exist.

If we pass from these general questions of administration to the economic question of the production and distribution of wealth, we shall find that many Radicals go half-way to Socialism. And here let me point out that my friend Mr. Bradlaugh is attacking a very crude presentment of Socialism when he defines it as "the theory and the scheme which denies all individual property, which denounces individual effort for individual gain, and affirms that society organised as the State should own all wealth, protect all labor, and compel the equal distribution of all produce. A Socialistic State would be a State in which everything would be held in common, in which the labor of each individual would be protected and controlled by the State, to which would belong all results of such labor." Socialism does not deny "all individual property"; it would leave a man in full possession of his share of the value he and his fellow-laborers had produced. It denounces "individual effort for individual gain" when the individual utilises other people's efforts for his individual gain; and it points out that when many co-operate to produce no one man should claim the common product as his. It does not affirm that the State should "own all wealth", but that it should own the raw material and the means of production. It does affirm that the State should protect all labor, and it affirms further that the present State performs that primary function extremely badly. It does not affirm that the State should compel the equal distribution of all produce, nor of any produce, but seeks to secure to the worker the value he creates, leaves him free to exchange the results of his labor as he will. Nor does the Socialist ask that "everything should be held in common", but that those things only shall be held in common the possession of which by individuals enables them to enslave their fellows, and to force others to work for their advantage. To say that Socialists desire to destroy all property because they would vest the ownership of land and capital in the community, is as misleading as it would be to say that Radicals desire to destroy all order because they say that legislative power should be vested in the representatives of the people and not in an autocratic sovereign. Take the numerous suggestions put forward by representative Socialists, such as Bebel, that men should be paid for their work by labor-notes, or by some symbol of exchange, representing the labor given by the individual. Those labor-notes would represent so much time given to labor. The recipient would own these notes; he might save them, spend them, waste them; one thing only he would not be able to do with them—force men to sell themselves to him and annex their labor for his own profit.

I have already pointed out that we do not propose that the labor of every individual citizen should be directed by a central body; but even were it true that such were our proposal, I fail to see that the liberty of the worker would be narrower then than it is now. Why would it be worse to have one's labor controlled by the State than to have it controlled by the individual employer? A workman does not control his labor now; he must sell it for what he can get for it. His labor is controlled by the individual manufacturer, who controls it for his own advantage; whereas the State would control it for the corporate advantage in which the worker would share. But it is, of course, not practicable that the State, as a whole, should direct and control the labor of each individual. For what is the State? It is the people, organised as a community. As a whole, the State could not control the labor of each citizen; but when the people are organised in groups of workers, each group can very well control its own labor, and elect its own superintendents, as well as elect such representatives as might be necessary to constitute boards of management to keep group in touch with group. The Trades Unions have in them the germs of the necessary organisation. If every miner were in the Miners' Union, then that union, with its branches in every coal district, would be the body which would immediately control the production of coal in a Socialist State. Can Radicals, who have fostered Trades Unions and urged the workers to combine, oppose a development of them? Can they, who have so preached self-reliance and self-government, maintain that men must always work for masters, and that they are not competent to control their own labor and to regulate their own production?

Again, the Socialist declaration that private property in land should be abolished is endorsed by the majority of Radicals in principle, however much some may falter in carrying it into practice. The evils that result to the community from the soil on which it lives being owned by a class are patent even to careless observation. We see the increase of a town population drive up rents, and the owners of the soil growing wealthier and wealthier without any exertion of theirs contributing to their swelling revenues. They are able to levy a cumulative tax on industry, and to grow fat in idleness while others grow lean in toil. And if we seek the reason why some should be placed in a position of such huge advantage, we often find that it is because they are at the end of a long line, at the beginning of which stands a man who got the land by force or fraud. And seeking further, we find that the laws protecting the monopoly are laws which were made by the people who profited by it, so that the laws by which landlords hold the land are laws made by landlords. It is as though a minority of thieves, getting the upper hand, made laws legalising robbery; and it is time that the people, now that legislative power is theirs, should repeal the laws which legalise wrong, and should assume the collective ownership of the soil. The State should be the only landowner.

It does not, however, follow from State ownership that the whole land of a country should be controlled from its metropolis. It would be better that municipalities should hold the land in towns, and local boards in agricultural districts, than that the State for landholding purposes should be concentrated too much, centralised too severely. If a municipality held the land on which a town was built, all rents would go into the municipal exchequer, and they would be used for the benefit of the town instead of for the enrichment of an idle landlord. Now, a good many Radicals are at one with Socialists on this point, and in what position is the Radical who is in favor of the State being the only landlord? He is a long way on the road to Socialism, half-way towards it at least, since Socialism demands the abolition of private property in land *and capital*. If the Radical already goes so far as to desire the abolition of private property in land, it is not wonderful that Socialists should look forward to his taking the other step, the abolition of private property in capital.

For the reasons which lead the Socialists to desire the abolition of private property in capital are cogent, and are such as must appeal to the unpropertied classes of the community. A man who does not inherit land or capital can only live by the sale of his labor, and he must sell his labor for what it will fetch. The price he can get for it depends on population—the number competing for work—and on the cost of living. If a man can earn a bare subsistence by the sale of his labor, he will sell it. Competition among employers may drive up the rate of wages for a while, for the profit made out of men's labor may be so great that it becomes worth while to "throw away a herring to catch a whale". But wage ever tends to fall to the cost of living, and will continue to do so as long as there are employers and employed. The amount of a man's wage is not fixed by the value he produces by his labor; the same value may be produced by each of two workers, and the wage paid may differ considerably. The boot and shoe trade in Northamptonshire offers an apt illustration of this bearing of the cost of living on wage. It is complained in the town of Northampton that much of the boot-and-shoe-making for which the district is famous is now being carried on in the villages round, because the goods can be produced there more cheaply than in the town. Now it is clear that the goods produced in the villages are as valuable as those produced in the town: the same amount of labor is put into them, and the same price obtained for them. If the value of men's work influenced their wage, the country workers would receive a wage equal to that paid in the town. But the wage varies with the cost of living. Rent is lower in the country, and living is cheaper, so a man will take less money for his labor, the wage duly sinking to subsistence level. And much above that level it can never permanently rise.

Going a step further, we can see that the production by the laborer of a much greater value than he receives as wage is the condition of his employment. The employer does not hire a man for his amusement; he hires him that he may make something out of him. The employers are often spoken of as the benefactors of labor, but this view is a decidedly topsy-turvey one. Is it not the laborer who benefits the employer, rather than the employer the laborer? The laborer works hard all his life for wage, and deems himself lucky if he saves enough to keep himself out of the workhouse in his old age and to bury him decently. The employer builds his grand house, and his stables, and his hothouses, and leaves a fortune made in trade to his heirs. On which side is the benefit? Which is the benefactor? Is it not labor which benefits the employer? labor which makes bare subsistence for itself and heaps up wealth for another. If one man is to make a profit, another man must make a loss. Wealth is only made by hard human labor, and the profit made by the employer is the measure of the loss suffered by the workmen. Granted that wages may be forced up a little by combination, yet so long as a profit is made out of the worker so long will he have less than he ought to have. It is said that employers work, and in so far as the employer contributes to the value of the product just so far has he also a right to share in the total value produced. Working employers have a right to remuneration, but the remuneration should be based on the value they add to the product, and should not consist of profit made by annexing part of the value made by others. As a matter of fact, a large number of the owners of capital do not work at all: they invest their capital, or have it invested for them, and they live on the interest they draw from it—mere idlers existing on the work of others. As long as one class can prey upon another, so long will it prey; and the propertied classes will live on the unpropertied for just so long as the latter will submit to the burden. Capital is made by labor, by associated labor, and can only exist where men co-operate for a common end; surely it is not unreasonable to demand that that which is produced by common labor shall be under common control. No individual should have the right to monopolise the result of associated labor for his own personal advantage, for his own personal gain. Under the system proposed by Socialism, in which the means of production would be under common control—that is, in which each trade would own for use the machinery needed in the trade—under that system only can be stopped the constant war between capital and labor, for under it co-operating, self-ruling workers would be substituted for masters and men.

I have already suggested that under Socialism each trade would form a Trade Union, each such Union controlling its own industry. These Unions will need to be kept in touch with each other by a central Industrial Board, to which each will elect a representative. A step has been taken towards making such a Board possible by the establishment, on Charles Bradlaugh's initiative, of a Labor Bureau, which will collate the statistics relating to the various trades, and will so render possible a regulation of industry where at present we have blind and aimless competition.

It is said that any regulation of industry means slavery; that the State will say to a man, go and do so and so. Not so. There is no reason why, under Socialism, a man should not be as free to choose his work as he is now. If there were too many in one particular trade then, as now, some would have to choose another. There might be a rush to one industry, and some would have to take other work; but the advantage would lie in the central Board, able to say where labor was wanted, so doing away with the heart-breaking tramp after work which is the lot of so many to-day.

Socialism is no wild scheme, no Utopia impossible of realisation. It is a carefully-reasoned scheme of production, distribution, and administration, which it is contended is better than the monopoly system of to-day. It would put an end to the war of classes, for it would substitute a community of workers for the present gradations of social rank. It would bid all healthy adults work, but it would also give to each leisure to enjoy. And since of all the political parties it is the Radicals only who claim liberty and equality for all, who admit no hereditary rights, who demand from all discharge of social duty, who base society on justice, not on privilege, who look to reason as guide, and not to authority, therefore it is to them that the Socialists must naturally turn for alliance, seeking to march with them against the common foe.

THE

SOCIALIST MOVEMENT.

BY

ANNIE BESANT.

[Reprinted from the "Westminster Review".]

LONDON:
FREETHOUGHT PUBLISHING COMPANY,
63, FLEET STREET, E.C.
1887.

PRICE THREEPENCE.

THE SOCIALIST MOVEMENT.

Some good-hearted people must have felt an uncomfortable thrill when they heard Professor Huxley declare that he would rather have been born a savage in one of the Fiji Islands than have been born in a London slum. The advantages of civilisation, from the slum point of view, must appear somewhat doubtful; and as a considerable part of the population of every large city live in the slums, the slum view has an importance of its own as a factor in the future social evolution. For it must be remembered that the slum population is not wholly composed of criminals and ne'er-do-weels—the "good-for-nothings" of Herbert Spencer. The honest workman and struggling seamstress live there cheek by jowl with the thief and and the harlot; and with the spread of education has arisen an inclination to question whether, after all, everything has been arranged quite as well as it might be in this best of all possible worlds. The question, Whether on the whole civilisation has been an advantage? has been a theme of academical discussion since Rousseau won the prize for an essay on "Has the restoration of the Sciences contributed to purify or to corrupt Manners?" and laid down the audacious thesis that riches gave birth to luxury and idleness, and from luxury sprang the arts, from idleness the sciences. But it has now changed its form, and has entered the arena of practical life: men are asking now, Is it rational that the progress of society should be as lopsided as it is? Is it necessary that, while civilisation brings to some art, beauty, refinement—all that makes life fair and gracious—it should bring to others drudgery, misery, degradation, such as no uncivilised people know; and these emphasised and rendered the bitterer by the contrast of what life is to many, the dream of what it might be to all? For Professor Huxley is right. The savage has the forest and the open sea, the joy of physical strength, food easily won, leisure sweet after the excitement of the chase; the civilised toiler has the monotonous drudgery of the stuffy workshop, the hell of the gin-palace for his pleasure-ground, the pandemonium of reeking court and stifling alley for his lullaby: civilisation has robbed him of all natural beauty and physical joy, and has given him in exchange—the slum. It is little wonder that, under these circumstances, there are many who have but scant respect for our social fabric, and who are apt to think that any change cannot land them in a condition worse than that in which they already find themselves.

The tendency to think of complete social change as a possible occurrence has come down to the present generation as an inheritance of the past. Old men still dwell fondly on the hopes of the "social missionaries" who were preaching when the men now of middle-age were born. Some even remember the experiments of Robert Owen and of his personal disciples, the hopes raised by New Lanark and Arbiston, the chill disappointment of New Harmony. The dream that glorified their youth has remained a sacred memory, and they have told how all might have been different had society been prepared in Owen's time for the fundamental change. And the great and far-reaching co-operative movement, born of Owen's Socialism, has kept "his memory green", and has prepared men to think of a possible future in which co-operation should wholly replace competition, and Owen's dream of universal brotherhood become a living reality. Such part of the energy of the Owenite Socialists as was not merged in co-operative activity was swamped in the sudden rush of prosperity that followed the repeal of the Corn Laws and the English triumph of Free Trade. Now that that rush is long over, and the old misery is on the workers once more, their minds turn back to the old schemes, and they listen readily to suggestions of a new social order.

The abnormally rapid multiplication characteristic of the very poor is at once constantly rendering the problem to be solved more difficult and more imperatively pressing.

Unhealthy conditions force the young into premature nubility; marriage takes place between mere lads and lasses; parenthood comes while father and mother are themselves legally infants; and the dwarfed, peaky little mortals, with baby frames and wizened faces, that tumble over each other in the gutters of the slums, are the unwholesome and unlovely products of the forcing-house of extreme poverty.

The spread of education and of religious scepticism has added the last touch necessary to make the poor ripe for social change. Ignorance is a necessary condition for prolonged submission to remediable misery. The School Boards are teaching the children the beauty of order, cleanliness, and decency, and are waking up in them desire for knowledge, hopes, and aspirations—plants unsuited for cultivation in the slums. They are sowing the seeds of a noble discontent with unworthy conditions, while at the same time they are developing and training the intelligence, and are converting aimless, sullen grumbling into a rational determination to understand the Why of the present, and to discover the How of change. Lastly, religious scepticism has enormously increased the value put upon the life which is. So long as men believed that the present life was the mere vestibule of an endless future, it was possible to bribe them into quiescence in misery by representing poverty as a blessing which should hereafter bring in its train the "kingdom of heaven". But now that many look on the idea of a life beyond the grave with doubt, and even with disbelief, this life has taken giant proportions in their eyes, and the human longing for happiness, which erstwhile fed on hopes of heaven, has fastened itself with passionate intensity on the things of earth.

Such is the soil, ploughed by misery, fertilised by education and scepticism, ready to receive and nourish the seed of social change.

While the soil has been thus preparing, the sowers who are to scatter the seed have been fashioning. Thoughtful persons have noted the regular cycle of alternate depression and inflation trodden by industrialism during the last century. At one time industry progresses "by leaps and bounds", employment is plentiful, wages high (as wages go), prices of coal and iron high, profits increase, and fortunes are rapidly built up. This inflation after a while passes away, and is succeeded by depression; "short time" is worked, wages are reduced, profits diminish, the "market is overstocked". This in its turn passes away, and temporary prosperity returns, to be after a while succeeded by another depression, and that by another inflation. But it is noticeable that the depressions become more acute and more prolonged as they return time after time, and that there is less elasticity of revival after each. The position of England in the world's markets becomes yearly one of diminished advantage; other nations raise their own coal and their own iron instead of buying from us, and as the competition of nations becomes keener, English trade can no longer monopolise the custom of the world. The radical weakness of our industrial system is thus becoming patent —no longer veiled, as it was during the first half of the century, by a monopoly which brought such enormous gains that the drain of wealth into a few hands was comparatively little felt. Now that there is so much less to divide, the unfairness of the method of division is becoming obvious.

Nor can we overlook, in tracing the fashioning of those who are to sow the seeds of change, the effect on English thought of the greatly increased communication with foreign countries, and especially with Germany. English religious thought has been largely influenced by the works of Strauss and Feuerbach; philosophic thought by those of Hegel, Kant, and Schopenhauer; scientific by the speculations of Goethe, the practical labors of Vogt, Büchner, and Haeckel. English insularity has been broken down in every domain of theoretical and speculative thought; it was inevitable that it should also be broken down in the domain of practical sociology, and that German proposals for social change should win the attention of English students of social problems. The works of Marx, Bebel, Liebknecht, and Engels have not reached any large number of English people; neither have those of Strauss, Hegel, and Kant. None the less in each case have they exercised a profoundly modifying influence on religious, philosophical, and sociological thought respectively; for, reaching a small band only, that band has in its turn influenced thought in the direction taken by itself, and has modified the views of very many who are unconscious of the change thus wrought in their own attitude towards progress. At the same time the German graft has been itself modified by the English stock, and English Socialism is beginning to take its own distinctive color; it is influenced by English traditions, race, habit, and methods of public procedure. It shows, at its best, the influence of the open-air of English political life, the tolerance of diversity of thought which is bred of free speech; it is less arrogant, less intolerant, than it is with Germans, or with those English who are most directly under German influence. In Germany the intolerance of oppression has caused intolerance of revolt; here the very power of the democracy has a tendency to sober its speech, and to make it take its own way in the quiet consciousness of its resistless strength. This peculiarity of English life must modify Socialism, and incline it to resort to methods of legislation rather than to methods of dynamite.

Nor has the effect of foreign thought been confined to the influence exerted by thinkers over thinkers, through the medium of the press. A potent worker for the internationalisation of thought has been silently busy for many years past. At first insular prejudices were broken down only for the wealthy and the nobles, when the "grand tour" was a necessary part of the education of the fine gentleman. Then the capitalist broke down national fences for his own gain, feeling himself nearer in blood to his foreign colleagues than to the workers in his own land; for, after all, common interests lie at the root of all fellow-feeling. And the capitalist abolished nationalism for himself: he hired Germans and Frenchmen for his counting-house work, finding them cheaper and better educated than English clerks; when his English wage-workers struck for better wages he brought over foreigners to take their place, so that he might live on cheap foreign labor while he starved the English into submission. The effect of foreign immigration and of foreign importation has not in the long run turned wholly to the advantage of the capitalist; for his foreign clerks and his foreign workers have fraternised with the English they were brought over to displace. They have taken part in club discussions; they have spread their own views; they have popularised in England the ideas current among workers on the Continent; they have made numbers of Englishmen acquainted with the solutions suggested abroad for social problems. Thus, the internationalism of the luxurious idle and of the wealthy capitalist has paved the way for the internationalism of the future—the internationalism of the proletariat, the internationalism of Socialism.

From this preliminary sketch of the conditions which make for a Socialist movement in England at the present time we must turn to an examination of the doctrines held and taught by the modern school, which claims to teach what is known as Scientific Socialism. The allegation, or even the proof, that modern civilisation is to a large extent a failure, is obviously not sufficient ground for a complete social revolution. Appeals to the emotions by means of word-pictures of the sufferings and degradation of the industrious poor, may rouse sympathy, and may even excite to riot, but can never bring about fundamental changes in society. The intellect must be convinced ere we can look for any wise movement in the direction of organic improvement; and while the passion of the ignorant has its revolutionary value, it is on the wisdom and foresight of the instructed that we must rely for the work of social reconstitution.

The first thing to realise is that the Socialist movement is an economic one. Despite all whirling words, and revolution fire, and poetic glamor, and passionate appeal, this one dry fact is the central one—Socialism rejects the present industrial system and proposes an exceedingly different one. No mere abuse can shake the Socialist; no mere calling of names can move him. He holds a definite economic theory—a theory which should neither be rejected without examination, nor accepted without study.

The preliminary stock objection which is often held to be sufficient to wave Socialism out of court is the statement that it is "against the laws of political economy". No statement could be more erroneous; though it may be pleaded in extenuation that the abuse levelled by ignorant Socialists at political economy has given excuse for supposing that it is in antagonism to Socialism. With political economy, as the science which deals with the nature, the production, and the distribution of wealth, Socialism can have no quarrel. Its quarrel is with the present industrial system, not with the science which points out the ascertained sequence of events under that system. Suppose a *régime* of avowed slavery: political economy, dealing with the production of wealth in such a state, would lay down how slaves might be worked to the best advantage—how most might be got out of them with least expenditure. But it would be irrational to attack political economy as brutal under such conditions; it would be the slave system which would be brutal, and blame of the science which merely dealt with the existent facts would be idle. The work of political economy is to discern and expound for any type of social system the best methods of producing and distributing wealth *under that system*; and it can as easily study and develop those methods under a *régime* of universal co-operation such as Socialism, as under a *régime* of universal competition such as the present. Socialism is in antagonism to the present system, and seeks to overthrow it; but only the ignorant and the thoughtless confound in their hatred the system itself, and the science that deals with its phænomena.

In truth, Socialism founds part of its disapproval of the present industrial system on the very facts pointed out by orthodox economists. It accepts Ricardo's "iron law of wages" and, recognising that wages tend to fall to the minimum on which the laborer can exist, it declares against the system of the hiring of workers for a fixed wage, and the appropriation of their produce by the hirer. It accepts Ricardo's theory of rent, with such modifications as are adopted by all modern economists. It assents to, and indeed insists on, the facts that all wealth is the result of labor applied to natural agents, that capital is the result of labor and abstinence, that in all save the most primitive forms of industry capital and labor—that is, the unconsumed result of past labor and present labor—are both necessary factors in the production of wealth.

Nor does Socialism challenge the accuracy of the deductions from the "laws of political economy" in a competitive system drawn by the trading community. That a man who desires wealth should buy in the cheapest market and sell in the dearest; that he should drive the hardest possible bargains; that in selling he should be guided by the maxim, *caveat emptor*; that in buying he should take advantage of the ignorance or the necessities of the seller; that the weakest should go the wall; that feeling should not interfere with business; that labor should be bought at the lowest possible price, and as much got out of it as may be; that trade morality differs from the morality of private life—all these maxims the Socialist regards as the evil fruits of the perpetuation among men of the struggle for existence: a struggle which, however inevitable among brutes, is from his point of view unworthy of human civilisation.

Recognising thus the unsatisfactory results which flow naturally and inevitably from the present system, Socialism proceeds to analyse the way in which wealth is produced and accumulated under it, to seek for the causes of the extreme wealth and extreme poverty which are its most salient characteristics.

Applying ourselves, then, to the study of the production of wealth, we find taking part therein three things—natural agents, capital, and labor. These, under the present system, are represented in England by three types—the landlord, the capitalist, and the proletarian. The transitional organisms need not detain us: the landlord who tills his land with his own hands, the capitalist who works in his own mill—these are exceptions; and we are concerned with the normal types. Abroad, the landlord pure and simple is comparatively rare. Of these three, the landlord owns the natural agents; no wealth can be produced without his consent. John Stuart Mill ("Principles of Political Economy", bk. ii., ch. xvi., sec. 1) remarks that "the only person, besides the laborer and the capitalist, whose consent is necessary to production, and who can claim a share of the produce as the price of that consent, is the person who, by the arrangements of society, possesses exclusive power over some natural agent". Given a person who, by possession of the natural agents from which wealth can be produced, can prevent the production of wealth by withholding the raw material, and you have a person who can successfully claim part of the wealth to be produced as a condition of allowing production to take place. He gains, by virtue of his position, wealth which one less fortunately placed can only acquire by prolonged labor. Nay, more; since many capitalists will compete for the raw material when it is advantageously situated, he will be able to obtain an ever higher price from the most eager bidder; as towns increase and trade develops, competition will drive the price up still higher; and this ever-mounting "rent", paid to the owner of the natural agents, will enrich the lucky possessor, however idle, ignorant, or useless he may be. Thus is produced a class which has a vested right to tax industry, and which taxes it in proportion to its success. Not an improvement can be effected, nor a railway constructed, nor a road made, without toll being first paid to the owner of the soil. The whole nation is at the mercy of a comparatively small class, so long as it consents to admit that this class has a right to own the ground on which the nation lives. Here is a point at which Socialism finds itself in direct antagonism to the present system of society. Socialism declares that natural agents ought not to be private property, and that no idle class should be permitted to stand between land and labor, and demand payment of a tax before it will permit the production of wealth. Socialism holds that the soil on which a nation is born and lives ought to belong to the nation as a whole, and not to a class within the nation; that the soil should be cultivated by individuals, or by co-operative groups, holding directly under the State—the "State" here meaning central organising body or district organising body, according as the organisation is communal or centralised. And here, among different Socialist schools, difference in detail manifests itself. All agree that the soil must in some fashion be controlled by the community, and the benefits derivable from it spread over the community. But some Socialists would have each commune practically independent, with the soil on which it lives vested in each; the agriculturists of the commune would form an organised body for cultivating the soil, and the agricultural products would be collected in the communal store, and thence distributed as each member of the commune had need of them. Nothing would here be recognised as "rent", since the total produce would pass under communal control. Other Socialists favor a system of more centralised management. But all agree that individual property in land must disappear, and that in the future land must not be used as an investment which is to bring in a profit in the shape of rent to some speculator or idler, but must be used for purposes of production for the general good, yielding food and raw materials for clothing and other necessaries of life, but profit in the shape of rent to no individual.

The extreme Radical school of politicians accepts the Socialist theory of land, and denounces private property in the soil as vigorously as does the Socialist. In fact, the Radical is a half-fledged Socialist—indignant as many would be at the description: he is in favor of the State being the landowner, but he boggles at the idea of the State being the capitalist. His attitude to the land is, however, an important factor in the Socialist movement, for it familiarises the national mind with the idea of the State absorbing the functions hitherto belonging to a class. The establishment of Land Courts, the fixing of judicial rents, the legal restrictions put on the "rights" of landlords—all these make for Socialism. M. Agathon de Potter, a well-known Continental writer, rejoices over the introduction of Mr. Charles Bradlaugh's Bill for expropriating landlords who keep cultivable land uncultivated, and for vesting the forfeited lands in the State, as a direct step towards Socialism. The shrinking of English politicians from the name does not prevent their advance towards the thing, and the Liberty and Property Defence League is justified in its view that politics are drifting steadily in a Socialist direction.

Pass we from the landlord who holds the natural agents to the capitalist who holds the means of production. What is capital, and how has it come into existence? Capital is any wealth which is employed for profit. On this there is no dispute. As Senior says: "Economists are agreed that *whatever* gives a profit is properly called capital". Now, as all wealth is the result of labor applied to natural agents, capital, being wealth, must have been so produced. But another factor has been at work; as Marshall says: it is "the result of labor *and abstinence*". Wherever there is capital there has been labor, and there has also been abstinence from consumption. But in studying the origin and the accumulation of capital, this remarkable historical fact stares us in the face—that capital is not found in the hands of the laborious and the abstemious, but is obtained by a process of confiscation of the results of labor and the imposition of privation on the laborious. On this John Stuart Mill has the following pregnant passage:

"In a rude and violent state of society it continually happens that the person who has capital is not the very person who has saved it, but someone who, being stronger, or belonging to a more powerful community, has possessed himself of it by plunder. And even in a state of things in which property was protected, the increase of capital has usually been, for a long time, mainly derived from privations which, though essentially the same with saving, are not generally called by that name, because not voluntary. The actual producers have been slaves, compelled to produce as much as force could extort from them, and to consume as little as the self-interest or the usually very slender humanity of their taskmasters would permit. ("Principles of Political Economy", bk. i., ch. v., sec. 5).

Capital always has been, and it always must be, obtained by the partial confiscation of the results of labor; that is, it must be accumulated by labor which is not paid for, or by labor of which the payment is deferred. In slave communities the slave-owner becomes a great capitalist by appropriating the total results of his slaves' toil, and returning to them only such small portion of it as suffices to keep the wealth-producers in capable working order. That is, the wealth produced *minus* the amount consumed by the producers, goes to the owner, and that part of it which he does not consume is laid by to be employed as capital. And it is worth noting that no considerable accumulation of capital was made, and no rapid progress in civilisation was possible, until slavery was introduced. In a low stage of evolution men will not deny themselves present for the sake of future enjoyment, nor incur present toil for the sake of future ease. But when, as was neatly said to me, the barbarian discovered that he could utilise his conquered enemy to much greater advantage by making him work than by merely eating him, civilisation had a chance. Slavery was, in truth, a necessary stage in social evolution; only by forced toil and forced privation was it possible to accumulate capital, and without capital no forms of complex industry are realisable. At the present time that which was done frankly and unblushingly in the slave *régime* is done under a veil of fine phrases, among which free contract, free laborer, and the like, play a striking part. But in reality the "free laborer" only obtains as wage such portion of the results of his labor as enables him to exist at the standard of living current for his class at the time, and the remainder of his produce goes to his employer. And too often this portion of his is not sufficient to keep him in capable working order, as is shown by the sombre fact that the average age of the hand-workers at death is far less than that of the idlers. For in truth the slave of the past had this advantage over the wage-worker of the present—that it was to his master's interest to keep the slave in high physical condition, and to prolong his working life; whereas it is to the modern employer's interest to get as much work out of the "free laborer" as is possible in a short time, and then to fling him aside as he begins to flag, and hire in his place a younger and more vigorous competitor, to be in his turn wrung dry and thrown away.

Before considering what Socialism would do with the capitalist, we must turn to the proletarian, his necessary correlative. A proletarian is a person who is possessed of labor-force, and of nothing else. He is the incarnation of the "labor" necessary for the production of wealth, the third factor in our trio. This type, in our modern society, is numerous, and is rapidly increasing. He is the very antithesis of the really free laborer, who works on his own raw material with his own instruments of production, and produces for his own subsistence. In the country the proletarian is born on somebody else's land, and as he grows up he finds himself owner of nothing except his own body. The raw material around him is owned by the landlord; the instruments of production are owned by the capitalist farmers. As he cannot live on his own labor force, which can only become productive in conjunction with raw material and means of production (capital), he must either sell it or starve. Nominally he may be free; in reality he is no more free than is the slave. The slave is free to refuse to work, and to take in exchange the lash, the prison, the grave; and such freedom only has the present proletarian. If he refuses to work, he must take the lash of hunger, the prison of the workhouse, and, on continued refusal, the actual gaol. Nor can he put his own price on this solitary property of his, his body—he must sell it at the market rate; and in some agricultural counties of England at the present time the market rate is from 7s. to 9s. a week. It is most significant of the bearing of the propertyless condition of the proletarian that many farmers object to the very slight improvement made in the laborer's position by his being permitted to rent at a high price a small allotment which he cultivates *for himself*. The ground of the farmer's objection is that even such small portion of freedom makes the laborer "too independent", and thereby drives up wages. To get the full advantage out of him, the proletarian must be wholly dependent for subsistence on the wages he earns. The town proletarian is in a similar position—neither land nor instrument of production is his; but he also has his labor force, and this he must sell, or he must starve.

We have arrived at the citadel of the Socialist position. Here is this unpropertied class, this naked proletariat, face to face with landlord and capitalist, who hold in their grip the means of subsistence. It must reach those means of subsistence or starve. The terms laid down for its acceptance are clear and decisive: "We will place within your hands the means of existence if you will produce sufficient to support us as well as yourselves, and if you will consent that the whole of your produce, over that which is sufficient to support you in a hardy, frugal life, shall be the property of us and of our children. If you are very thrifty, very self-denying, and very lucky, you may be able to save enough out of your small share of your produce to feed yourself in your old age, and so avoid falling back on us. Your children will tread the same mill-round, and we hope you will remain contented with the position in which Providence has placed you, and not envy those born to a higher lot." Needless to say, the terms are accepted by a proletariat ignorant of its own strength, and the way to profit is open to landlord and capitalist. The landlord, as we have seen, obtains his share of the gains by taxing the capitalist through raising his rent. The capitalist finds his profit in the difference between the wage he pays and the value of the produce of his hired workers. The wage is fixed by the competition for employment in the labor market, and limited in its downward tendency by the standard of living. The minimum wage is that on which the worker can exist, however hardly. For less than this he will not work. Every shilling above this is fought over, and wage rises and falls by competition. At every stage of their relationship there is contest between employer and employed. If the wage is paid for a fixed day's work—as in nearly every trade—the employer tries to lengthen the day, the employed to shorten it; the longer the day, the greater the production of "surplus value"—*i.e.*, of the difference between the wage paid and the value produced. The employer tries to increase surplus value by pressing the workers to exertion; they lessen exertion in order not to hasten the time of their discharge. The employer tries still to increase surplus value by supplanting male labor with female and child labor at lower wages. The men resist such introduction, knowing that the ultimate result is to increase the amount taken by capital and to lessen that obtained by labor.

Now the Socialist alleges that these antithetical interests can never be reconciled while capital and labor are the possessions of two distinct classes. He points to the results brought about by the capitalist class while it was left unshackled by the State. The triumph of capitalism, and of *laisser-faire* between employers and employed, was from 1764 to 1833. During that time not only adults but young children were worked from fifteen to sixteen hours a day, and the production of surplus value was enormous. The huge fortunes of the Lancashire "cotton-princes" were built up by these overtasked, quickly worn-out workers. The invention of machinery centupled man's productive power, and its benefits were monopolised by a comparatively small class; while those who made the wealth festered in closely crowded courts, those who appropriated the wealth luxuriated in country seats; one side of industrialism is seen in the Lancashire mansions, pleasure-grounds, and hothouses; the other in the reeking slums within the sound of the factory bells. Under a saner system of production, the introduction of machinery would have lightened toil, shortened the hours of necessary labor, and spread abundance where there was want. Under capitalistic industrialism it has built up huge fortunes for a few, and has reduced thousands to conditions of insanitary living and dreary degradation, worse than anything the world has hitherto known. It has poisoned our rivers, polluted our atmosphere, marred the beauty of our country's face, bestialised large numbers of our people. Improvements in machinery, which should be hailed with joy, are regarded with dread by large classes of workers, because they will throw numbers out of work, and reduce men, who were skilled laborers with the old machinery, into the ranks of the unskilled. True, the result of the introduction of machinery has been to cheapen—in consequence of competition among capitalists—many commodities, especially articles of clothing. But this effect is little felt among the laboring classes. They can buy perhaps three coats where they used to buy one, but the easily worn-out shoddy, thought good enough for clothes sold in poor quarters, is but a poor exchange for the solid hand-made stuffs worn by their ancestors.

What, then, is the remedy proposed by Socialism? It is to deal with capital as it deals with land; to abolish the capitalist as well as the landlord, and to bring the means of production, as well as the natural agents on which they are used, under the control of the community.

Capital is, as we have seen, the result of unpaid labor; in a complex system like our own it is the result of co-operative—that is, of socialised—labor. It has been found by experience that division of labor increases productive ability, and in all forms of industry numbers now co-operate to turn out the finished product. In each commodity is embodied the labor of many workers, and the socialisation of labor has reached a very advanced stage. But while industrialism has been socialised in its aspect of labor, it has remained individualistic in its aspect of capital; and the results of the combined efforts of many are appropriated to the advantage of one, and when the one has exhausted his power of consumption he retains the remaining results, and employs them for the further enslavement and exploitation of labor. Thus labor constantly adds new links to the chain which fetters it, and is ever increasing the capital which, let out at interest by its owners, becomes ever a heavier tax upon itself. Socialism contends that these unconsumed results of socialised labor ought not to pass into the hands of individuals to be used by them for their own profit; but should pass either into the industrial funds of the several trades that produce them, or into a central industrial exchequer. In either case, these funds created by past labor would be used for the facilitation of present and future labor. They would be available for the introduction of improved machinery, for the opening up of new industries, for the improvement of means of communication, and for similar undertakings. Thus, in a very real sense, capital would become only the deferred payment of labor, and the whole results of toil would be constantly flowing back upon the toilers. Under such conditions, fixed capital or plant would, like land, be held for purposes of use by the workers who used it. Its replacement would be a constant charge on the commodities it helped to produce. A machine represents so much human labor; that embodied labor takes part in producing the finished commodity as much as does the palpable labor of the human worker who superintends the machine; that worker does not produce the whole value added in the factory to the material brought into it, and has no claim to that whole value. The wear and tear of the machine is an offset, and must be charged on the products, so that when the machine is worn out there may be no difficulty in its replacement. Under such conditions also the distinction between employers and employed would disappear. All would be members of industrial communities, and the necessary foremen, superintendents, organisers, and officers of every kind, would be elected as the officers of trades unions are elected at the present time.

Poverty will never cease so long as any class or any individuals have an interest in the exploitation of others. While individuals hold capital, and other individuals cannot exist unless that capital is used for their employment, the first class will prey upon the second. The capitalists will not employ unless they can "make a profit" out of those they hire to work for them; that is, unless they pay them less than the value of the work produced. But if one man is to have value for which he has not worked, another must have less than the value of his work; and while one class grows wealthy on unpaid labor, another must remain poor, giving labor without return. Socialism would give to each return for labor done, but it recognises no claim in the idle to grow fat on the produce of the industrious.

Interest on capital, paid to individuals, has—as is obvious from the foregoing—no place in Socialism. Strongly as Socialism protests against the whole system of which landlords and capitalists form an integral part, it reserves its uttermost reprobation for the theory which justifies a class of the latter in living solely on money drawn as interest on investments. If a man possesses three or four thousand pounds he can invest them, and live all his life long on the interest without ever doing a stroke of honest work, and can then bequeath to some one else the right to live in idleness; and so on in perpetuity. Money in the capitalist system is like the miraculous oil in the widow's cruse—it can always be spent and never exhausted. A man in sixty years will have received in interest at five per cent. three times his original fortune, and although he may have spent the interest, and thus have spent every penny of his fortune three times over, he will yet possess his fortune as large as it was when he began. He has consumed in commodities three times the sum originally owned, and yet is not one penny the worse. Other people have labored for him, fed him, clothed him, housed him, and he has done nothing in exchange. The Socialist argument against this form of interest lies in a nutshell: a man earns £5; he gives labor for which he receives in exchange a power of possession over £5 worth of commodities; he desires only to consume £1 worth now, and to defer the consumption of the remaining £4. He buys his £1 worth of commodities, and considers himself repaid for the fifth portion of his work by possessing and consuming these. But he expects to put out his saved £4 at interest, and would consider himself hardly used if, fourteen years hence, when he desired to exercise his power of consumption, deferred for his own convenience, that power had not increased although he had done nothing to increase it. Yet it can only be increased by other people's labor being left unpaid for, while he is paid twice over for his; and this arrangement the Socialist stamps as unjust. So long as capital remains in the hands of individuals, interest will be demanded by them for its use, and will be perforce paid; and so long also will exist an idle class, which will consume without producing, and will remain a burden on the industrious, who must labor to support these as well as themselves, and must produce sufficient for all.

Now, Socialism aims at rendering impossible the existence of an idle class. No healthy adult but will have to work in exchange for the things he requires. For the young, freedom from labor; they have to prepare for life's work. For the aged, freedom from labor: they have worked, and at eventide should come rest. For the sick also, freedom from labor; and open hospitals for all, without distinction of class, where tendance and all that skill can do shall be at the service of each. But for the strong and the mature, no bread of idleness, no sponging upon other people. With division of labor will come also division of leisure; the disappearance of the languid lady, full of *ennui* from sheer idleness, will entail the disappearance of the overworked slavey, exhausted from unending toil; and there will be two healthy women performing necessary work, and enjoying full leisure for study, for art, for recreation, where now are the over-lazy and the over-driven.

In thus condemning the existence of an idle class, Socialism does not assail all the individuals who now compose it. These are not to blame for the social conditions into which they have been born; and it is one of the most hopeful signs of the present Socialist movement, that many who are working in it belong to the very classes which will be abolished by the triumph of Socialist principles. The man who has inherited a fortune, and has embraced Socialism, would do no good by throwing it away and plunging into the present competitive struggle; all he can do is to live simply, to utilise his position of advantage as a pedestal on which to place his advocacy of Socialism, and to employ his money in Socialist propaganda.

It is feared by some that the success of the Socialist movement would bring about the crushing of individualism and an undue restriction of liberty. But the Socialist contends that the present terrible struggle for existence is the worst enemy of individualism, and that for the vast majority individuality is a mere phrase. Exhausting toil and ever-growing anxiety, these crush out individuality, and turn the eager promising lad into the harassed drudge of middle age. How many capable brains are wasted, how many original geniuses lost to the nations they might illuminate, by the strife for mere livelihood? The artist fritters away his genius in "pot-boilers"; the dramatist writes down to the piece that will "pay", and harnesses his delicate fancy into coarse burlesque full of wretched witticisms; in the stress of the struggle to live, patient study and straining after a great ideal become impossible. Individualism will only develop fully when Socialism has lifted off all shoulders the heavy burden of care, and has given to all leisure to think and to endeavor.

Nor is the fear of undue restriction of liberty better founded than that of the crushing out of individualism. One kind of liberty, indeed, will be restricted—the liberty to oppress and to enslave other people. But with this exception liberty will be increased. Only the very wealthy are now free. The great majority of people must work, and their choice of work is very limited. The poor must take what work they can get, and their complaint is not that they are compelled to work, but that they often cannot get work to do. In satisfying the complex wants of the civilised human being there is room for all the most diverse capacities of work; and if it be said that there are unpleasant kinds of work that must be done, which none would willingly undertake, it may be answered that those kinds of work have to be done now, and that the compulsion of the community would not be a greater restriction of personal liberty than the present compulsion of hunger; and further, that it would be easy to make a short period of unpleasant toil balance a long period of pleasant; and that it would be far better to have such tasks divided among a number, so that they would press very lightly upon each, than have them, as now, pushed on to a comparatively few, whose whole lives are brutalised by the pressure. The very strictest organisation of labor by the community that can be imagined, would be to the great majority far less oppressive than the present system, for at the worst, it would but control an extremely small portion of each working day, and would leave the whole of the rest of the existence free, to be used at the pleasure of the individual, untrammelled by anxiety and harassing care for the mere necessaries of life. The pride in skill, the stimulus of honorable ambition, the pleasure of success, all these would be present, as they are to-day; but instead of being the privilege of the few, they would brighten the life of all.

A profound moral impulse really underlies the whole of the Socialist movement. It is a revolt against the callous indifference of the majority in the "comfortable classes" to the woful condition of large numbers of the workers. It is an outburst of unselfish brotherhood, which cannot bear to sit at ease while others suffer, which claims to share the common human lot, and to bear part of the burden now pressing with crushing weight on the shoulders of the poor. It detests the theory that there must always be hewers of wood and drawers of water for a luxurious class, and proclaims that human degradation lies in idle living, not in earnest work. It would have all work, that all may have leisure, and would so distribute the necessary work of the world that none may be crushed by it, but that all may be disciplined. And this very outburst of human brotherhood is in itself a proof that society is evolving Socialismwards, and that the evolution of humanity is reaching a stage in which sympathy is triumphing over selfishness, and the desire for equality of happiness is becoming a potent factor in human conduct. The Socialist ideal is one which could not meet with wide acceptance if humanity were not marching towards its realisation.

On one matter the Socialist movement, both abroad and at home, has set itself in opposition to science and to right reason—*e.g.*, on the law of population. It is easy to see how this opposition has arisen, and it may be hoped that when Socialists in general disentangle the scientific statement of facts from Malthus' unwise applications of them, Socialism and prudential restraint will be seen to be indissolubly united. Malthus accurately pointed out that population has a tendency to increase beyond the means of subsistence; that as it presses on the available means, suffering is caused; and that it is kept within them by what he termed "positive checks"—*i.e*, a high death-rate, especially among the children of the poor, premature death from disease, underfeeding, etc. The accuracy of his statement has been proved up to the hilt by Charles Darwin, who describes with abundant illustrations the struggle for existence—a struggle which is the direct result of the fact stated in the law of population, of the tendency of all animated things to increase beyond their food supply; this has led, and still leads, to the survival of those who are fittest for the conditions of the struggle. Unhappily, Malthus added to his scientific exposition some most unfortunate practical advice; he advised the poor not to marry until, practically, they had reached middle life. The poor felt, with natural indignation, that in addition to all their other deprivations they were summoned by Malthus to give up the chief of the few pleasures left to them, to surrender marriage, to live in joyless celibacy through the passion-season of life, to crush out all the impulses of love until by long repression these would be practically destroyed. Under such circumstances it is little wonder that "Malthusianism" became a word hated by the poor and denounced by those who sympathised with them. It is true that the advice of Malthus as to the putting off of marriage has been and is very widely followed by the middle classes; but it is perfectly well known that the putting off of marriage does not with them mean the observance of celibacy, and the shocking prostitution which is the curse of every Christian city is the result of the following of the advice of Malthus so far as marriage is concerned. It is obvious that Malthus ignored the strength of the sexual instinct, and that the only possible result of the wide acceptance of his teaching would be the increase of prostitution, an evil more terrible than that of poverty. But the objection rightly raised to the practical teaching of Malthus ought not to take the form of assailing the perfectly impregnable law of population, nor is it valid against the teachings of Neo-Malthusians, who advise early marriage and limitation of the family within the means of existence.

The acceptance of this doctrine is absolutely essential to the success of Socialism. Under a system in which children are forced to labor, they may begin to "keep themselves" at a very early age; but under a Socialist system, where education will occupy childhood and youth, and where old age is to be free from toil, it will soon be found that the adult working members will not permit an unlimited increase of the mouths which they have to fill. Facilitate production as we may, it will always take more hours to produce the necessaries of life for families of ten or twelve than for families of three or four. The practical enforcement of the question will probably come from the women; highly educated women, full of interest in public work and taking their share in public duty, will not consent to spend year after year of their prime in nothing but expecting babies, bearing babies, and suckling babies. They will rebel against the constant infliction of physical discomfort and pain, and will insist on the limitation of the family as a condition of marriage. The sooner this is recognised by Socialists the better, for at present they waste much strength by attacking a doctrine which they must sooner or later accept.

A glance backward over the history of our own country, since the Reform Bill of 1832 opened the gate of political power to those outside the sacred circle of the aristocracy, will tell how an unconscious movement towards Socialism has been steadily growing in strength. Our Factory Acts, our Mines Regulation Acts, our Education Acts, our Employers' Liability Acts, our Land Acts—all show the set of the current. The idea of the State as an outside power is fading, and the idea of the State as an organised community is coming into prominence. In the womb of time the new organism is growing: shall the new birth come in peace or in revolution, heralded by patient endeavor or by roar of cannon? Who can tell? But this one thing I know, that come it will, whether men work for it or hinder; for all the mighty, silent forces of evolution make for Socialism, for the establishment of the Brotherhood of Man.

CATALOGUE

OF

BOOKS AND PAMPHLETS,

SOLD BY

ROBERT FORDER,

28, STONECUTTER STREET, Farringdon Street,

LONDON, E.C.

ORDERS TO THE VALUE OF ONE SHILLING AND UPWARDS, SENT POST FREE, EXCEPT WHEN OTHERWISE STATED. CHEQUES AND POSTAL ORDERS SHOULD BE CROSSED AND MADE PAYABLE TO R. FORDER.

ALLBUTT, H. A., M.R.C.P.E., L.S.A., etc.

	s.	d.
The Wife's Handbook: How a woman should order herself during pregnacy, in the lying-in room, and after delivery; with hints on important matters necessary to be known by married women. 160th thousand. Limp cloth, 9d.: in paper covers,	0	6
Le Livre de l'Epouse. A French translation of the Wife's Handbook	0	10
——Trial before the General Medical Council of Great Britain, Nov. 23, 24 and 25, 1887, for publication of the *Wife's Handbook* "at so low a price"	0	3
Artificial Checks to Population: is the popular teaching of them infamous?	0	3
Disease and Marriage. By post, 1/9	1	6

ALLINSON, Dr. T. R.

	s.	d.
Medical Essays. In four books, each	1	0
Hygienic Medicine: or the Only Rational Way of Treating Disease	1	0
Diet and Digestion	0	6
Consumption	0	6
Rheumatism and Rheumatic Affections	0	6
Wholesome Cookery	0	1
Complete Works; *cloth*	8	6

ANONYMOUS.

	s.	d.
Will Shakespeare, Tom Paine, Bob Ingersoll and Charlie Bradlaugh	0	6
One Hundred and One Questions, to which the Orthodox are earnestly requested to give Answers	0	1
The Devil's Visit: Why he came, What he said, Why he left, and the Present he sent. A Poem for the times. 418 pp., *cloth*...	4	0
Freethought Leaflets, assorted, per 100, by post, 7½d. ...	0	6
The Bible and the Bung. A Freethought Lyric, *on card* ...	0	½
Sweet By and Bye ,, ,, ,, ...	0	½
Freethought Gleanings	0	1
Joseph and his Brethren. A Satirical Poem; illustrated; post free	0	3

AVELING, E. B., D.Sc.

	s.	d.
Theoretical and Practical General Biology; *cloth*	2	0
Darwin Made Easy. Three Essays: The Origin of Man; Monkeys, Apes and Men: The Darwinian Theory. *cloth*	1	0
Gospel of Evolution	0	1
The Student's Darwin; *cloth*	5	0
Biological Discoveries and Problems; *cloth*	1	0
Darwinism and Small Families	0	1
Essays; *cloth*	1	0
Physiological Tables	1	0
Botanical Tables	1	0
The Bookworm and other Sketches	0	6

BARKER, SAMUEL, M.D.

	s.	d.
Remarks on the Only True Foods for Infants and Children ...	0	6

BONSER, T. O.

	s.	d.
The Right to Die: an Argument in Favor of Suicide... ...	0	1

BESANT, ANNIE.

The Freethinker's Text-Book. Part II. "On Christianity." Section 1.—"Christianity: its Evidences Unreliable." Section 2.—"Its Origin Pagan." Section 3.—"Its Morality Fallible." Section 4.—"Condemned by its History." *Cloth* 3 6

History of the Great French Revolution. Three Courses of Lectures. First Series, cloth, 2s. Second Series, 9d. Third Series, 9d. In 1 vol. cloth 3 6

Light, Heat, and Sound. Illustrated. In three parts, 6d. each. Complete, *cloth* 2 0

Social and Political Essays, Containing: Disestablish the Church, or Sins of the Church of England; Sin and Crime: their nature and treatment; Ethics of Punishment, Legalisation of Female Slavery in England; Force no remedy; England's Jubilee Gift to Ireland; The Transvaal; Egypt, a protest against the War; The Story of the Soudan; Gordon Judged out of his own Mouth; Civil and Religious Liberty, with some Hints taken from the French Revolution: The Political Status of Women; English Republicanism; Liberty, Equality, and Fraternity; Landlords, Tenant Farmers, and Laborers; The English Land System; Eyes and Ears. *Cloth* 3 6

Essays on Socialism. Containing: The Redistribution of Political Power; The Evolution of Society; Modern Socialism; Why I am a Socialist; Radicalism and Socialism; The Socialist Movement. *Cloth* 2 6

Theological Essays and Debates. Containing: Atheism and its Bearing on Morals (Debate); The Teachings of Christianity (Debate); Roots of Christianity, or the Christian Religion before Christ; The Christian Creed; Life, Death, and Immortality; The World and its Gods; A World without God; Woman's Position according to the Bible; Christian Progress; Fruits of Christianity; The Gospel of Christianity and the Gospel of Freethought; Blasphemy; God's Views on Marriage; The Gospel of Atheism; Why I do not believe in God; Is the Bible Indictable? Biblical Biology; The Natural History of the Christian Devil; Is Christianity a Success? *Cloth* 5 0

Legends and Tales (*Young Folks' Library*). Contents:—Legends: 1. Ganga, the River Maid. 2. The Stealing of Persephone. 3. The First Roses. 4. The Drowning of the World. 5. A Curious Adventure. 6. Drawn from the Waters. 7. The Wandering Jew. Tales:—1. Hypatia. 2. Giordano Bruno. *Cloth*, attractively bound, illustrated 1 0

BESANT, ANNIE, Continued.

Disestablish the Church, or Sins of the Church of England. A *Vade Mecum* for Liberationists, full of details about Tithes, "Church" Revenues, Persecuting Laws, attitude of the Church towards Education, the Slavery Question, etc., etc. Neatly bound in cloth, gilt lettered, with Index of Contents 1 0

DEBATES—

The Jesus of the Gospels and The Influence of Christianity on the World. Two nights' Debate with the Rev. A. HATCHARD 1 0

Atheism and its bearing on Morals. Written Debate with Rev. G. F. Handel Rowe, of Halifax 0 6

The Teachings of Christianity. Written Debate with Rev. G. F. Handel Rowe, of Halifax 0 6

Is Socialism Sound? Four nights' Debate with G. W. Foote. Papers covers, 1s. *Cloth*, on superior paper 2 0

Socialism: For and Against. Written debate with Charles Bradlaugh 0 4

Socialism v. Individualism. A debate with F. Miller ... 0 2

PAMPHLETS—

Why I became a Theosophist 0 4
Theosophy and its Evidences 0 3
Roots of Christianity; or The Christian Religion before Christ 0 6
Life, Death, and Immortality 0 2
The World and its Gods 0 3
A World without God. Reply to Miss F. P. Cobbe 0 3
Woman's Position according to the Bible 0 1
Christian Progress 0 2
Fruits of Christianity 0 2
The Gospel of Christianity and the Gospel of Freethought ... 0 2
The Christian Creed. Parts I. and II., each 0 6
God's views on Marriage 0 2
The Gospel of Atheism 0 2
Why I do not believe in God 0 3
Is the Bible Indictable? 0 2
Biblical Biology 0 1
The Myth of the Resurrection. Tenth Thousand 0 1
Why should Atheists be Persecuted? 0 1
The Natural History of the Christian Devil 0 1
Is Christianity a Success? 0 1
Sins of the Church. In 8 numbers, each (16 pp.) 0 1
Do. do. Cloth, with index 1 0
Do. do. Part I. (6 numbers) 0 6
The Ethics of Punishment 0 1

BESANT, ANNIE, Continued.

	s.	d.
The True Basis of Morality. A Plea for Utility as the Standard of Morality. Seventh Thousand	0	2
Sin and Crime: their nature and Treatment	0	3
Auguste Comte. Biography of the great French Thinker, with Sketches of his Philosophy, his Religion, and his Sociology. Being a short and convenient *résumé* of Positivism for the general reader	0	6
The Trades Union Movement	0	4
Legalisation of Female Slavery in England	0	1
The Physiology of Home—No. 1, "Digestion"; No. 2, "Organs of Digestion"; No. 3, "Circulation"; No. 4, "Respiration"; together in neat wrapper	0	4
Electricity and its Modern Applications, in wrapper ...	0	4
Eyes and Ears	0	3
Modern Socialism	0	6
Why I am a Socialist	0	1
Radicalism and Socialism	0	3
The Socialist Movement (From *Westminster Review*) ...	0	3
The Evolution of Society	0	3
The Redistribution of Political Power	0	4
Gordon judged out of his own mouth	0	2
Liberty, Equality, and Fraternity	0	1
Landlords, Tenant Farmers, and Laborers	0	1
The English Land System	0	1
English Marseillaise, with Music	0	1
English Republicanism	0	1
The Political Status of Woman. A Plea for Women's Rights	0	2
Civil and Religious Liberty, with some Hints taken from the French Revolution. Sixth Thousand	0	3
England's Jubilee Gift to Ireland	0	1
The Transvaal	0	1
Egypt. A Protest against the War. 2nd edition	0	2
The Story of the Soudan	0	1
Free Trade *v.* "Fair" Trade—5 lectures: England before the Repeal of the Corn Laws"; "The History of the Anti-Corn Law Struggle"; Labour and Land: their burdens, duties, and rights"; "What is really Free Trade?" The Landlords' Attempt to Mislead the Landless." In paper cover, with Appendix	0	6
The Law of Population. Its consequences and its bearing upon human conduct and morals. This work is now withdrawn from circulation, and will not be reprinted. A few copies left, in *cloth covers,* post free	1	2
Theosophy and the Law of Population. Being Mrs. Besant's reasons for withdrawing from circulation her famous work "The Law of Population."		
1875 to 1891: A Fragment of Autobiography	0	2

BRADLAUGH, CHARLES.

	s.	d.
A fac-simile reprint of the late Mr. Bradlaugh's first pamphlet entitled, "A few Words on the Christian Creed." Originally issued in 1848.	0	2

For C. Bradlaugh's works see special catalogue.

BÜCHNER, PROF. LUDWIG, M.D.

Mind in Animals. Translated by Annie Besant; *cloth* ...	5	0
Force and Matter; or the Principles of the Natural Order of the Universe, with a system of Morality based thereon. Newly translated from the 15th German Edition. Portrait and Biography, *cloth gilt*	8	0
The Influence of Heredity on Free-will	0	2

CAMBRIDGE GRADUATE, (A.)

Twenty-four proofs that the Bible is not the Word of God ...	0	1

CATTELL, CHARLES C.

Thoughts for Thinking, from the Literature of all Ages ...	1	0
Against Christianity: showing its Theory Incredible and its Practise Impossible	0	6
The Religion of this Life	0	2
The Second Coming of Christ	0	2
Recollections of Charles Bradlaugh	0	1

CARLILE, RICHARD.

A Manual of Freemasonry, *cloth gilt*	2	6

"CELSUS."

Bible Bestialities, and Filth from the Fathers. With introduction by Lucianus	0	6

C. N.

What is Religion? A vindication of Freethought	1	0

COLLINS, W. W.

Geology and the Bible	0	1
Bible Biographies—Adam (with portrait)	0	1
Life and Death: an examination of the question—Does man survive physical death?	0	2
Law and God	0	3

COOPER, ROBERT.

The Immortality of the Soul Philosophically Considered. Seven Lectures 0 6

COOPER, R. A.

Free Railway Travel. A proposal that the state should acquire and maintain the Railways, making them free to the public like the Highways 0 6

COURTNEY, H. L.

Positive Agnosticism, or the New Gospel of Hylo-Idealism ... 0 3

DALTON, H. R. S., B.A., (Oxon.)

The Education of Girls 0 6
Ish's Charge to Women 0 4
Religion and Priestcraft 0 2

DRAPER, J. W., M.D., LL.D.

The Conflict between Religion and Science; *cloth* 5 0

DOCTOR OF MEDICINE (A).

The Elements of Social Science; or Physical, Sexual and Natural Religion. An exposition of the true cause and only cure of the three primary social evils—Poverty, Prostitution and Celibacy. 604 pp., *cloth* 3 0

DREW, MENA, (Miss).

Hints on Nursing; with a Preface by Dr. Allbutt 0 6
Monthly Nursing 0 6

DRYSDALE, C. R., M.D.

Vegetarian Fallacies 0 2
The Cause of Poverty 0 1
The Length of Life of Total Abstainers and Moderate Drinkers Compared 0 2

DUPUIS, C. F.

On the Connection of Christianity with Solar Worship. Translated by T. E. Partridge 1

DYMOND, C., F.S.A., and BROADHURST-NICHOLS, Rev. J.

The Practical Value of Christianity. Prize Essays, for and against 1 0

EADON, S., M.A., M.D., LL.D.

A Few Facts Relative to the Antiquity of Man; with an Appendix from an Astronomical Standpoint 0 2

ELLIOTT, F. J., M.R.A.C., F.H.A.S.

The Land Question: Its Examination and Solution, from an Agricultural point of view. Published at 5/-
Reduced to [Postage, 4½d.] 1 0

FOOTE, G. W., and G. BERNARD SHAW.

Two Night's Debate on the Eight Hour's Question; 77 pp.... 0 6

FORDER, R.

"There was War in Heaven" (Rev. xii. 7), a Satirical Infidel Sermon 0 1
St. Agnes and St. Bridget, and their Pagan Prototypes ... 0 1

GASKELL, G. A.

The Futility of Pecuniary Thrift as a means to General Well-being 0 2
Social Control of the Birth-rate and Endowment of Mothers 0 2

GOULD, F. J.

The Agnostic Island: a Novel 1 0

HARTMANN, EDWARD Von.

The Religion of the Future. Translated from the German by Ernest Dare; *cloth* 2 0

HARDAKER, W.

(Translated by) Old Thoughts for New Thinkers. Selections from the "Pensées Philosophiques" of Diderot ... 0 1

"HISTORICUS."

The Lords and what they have done 0 6

HITHERSAY, R., & G. ERNEST.

Life of Saladin 0 6

HUGO, VICTOR.

Oration on Voltaire 0 1

HOWELL, MISS CONSTANCE.

A Biography of Jesus Christ: *cloth* 1 6
The After Life of the Apostles; *cloth* 1 6
A History of the Jews; *cloth* 1 6
The above works were written for young Freethinkers.

HOLYOAKE, G. J.

The Trial of Theism; Accused of Obstructing Secular Life; *cloth, gilt lettered,* pub. at 4/-; [Postage 3d.] 2 6
What would Follow the Effacement of Christianity? ... 0 6
The Last Trial for Atheism in England: a Fragment of an Autobiography. Pub. at 1/6, post free 0 8
The Principles of Secularism Illustrated, post free 0 4
The Logic of Death 0 1
New Ideas of the Day 0 1

"HUMANITAS."

Jacob the wrestler, *cloth* 2 6
Jacob the wrestler, *paper* 2 0
The most exhaustive criticism of Jacob that has ever been written.
Thoughts upon Heaven 0 6
Is God the First Cause?... ... ... 0 6
Christ's Temptation 0 6
Charles Bradlaugh and the Irish Nation 0 6
Socialism a Curse... ... ... 0 3
A Fish in Labor, or Jonah and the Whale 0 3
Against Agnosticism 0 2
Charles Bradlaugh and the Oath Question 0 2
How Charles Bradlaugh was treated by House of Commons 0 2
The Follies of the Lord's Prayer Exposed 0 2
Against Socialism... ... ... 0 1
God: Being a brief statement of Arguments against Agnosticism... ... ... 0 6

HUME, DAVID.

On Miracles. With an Appendix, &c., by J. M. Wheeler ... 0 3
The Natural History of Religion. Complete and unexpurgated Edition, with the original notes, and an Introduction by J. M. Robertson ; *cloth* 1 0
Dialogues concerning Natural Religion. Originally issued in two 1/- parts, now complete in one volume. 1 0

HUXLEY, Prof. T. H., (F.R.S)

Possibilities and Impossibilities ; an Essay on Miracles ... 0 3

HYNDMAN, H. M.

Booth's Book Refuted 0 1
The Indian Famine and the Crisis in India ; pub. at 1/- ... 0 3

INDIAN OFFICER, AN.

A Voice from the Ganges ; or the True Source of Christianity. In *cloth*, 1/6 ; in *paper covers* 1 0

INGERSOLL, COL. ROBERT G.

The Three Philanthropists 0 2
True Religion 0 2
Humanity's Debt to Thomas Paine 0 2
Creeds and Spirituality 0 1
Christ and Miracles 0 1
Salvation Here and Hereafter 0 1
Modern Thinkers ; or the Spirit of the Age 0 1
Col. Ingersol at Home. Biographical Notes, Occasional Utterances, Characteristics 0 1

JANES, LEWIS, G.

A Study of Primitive Christianity ; *cloth* 6 0

JANES, A.

A Practical Introduction to Shorthand... ... ... 0 1
Shorthand without Complications : a complete guide to verbatim Reporting 1 0

JONES, L. A. ATHERLEY, M.P.

The Miners' Handy Book to the Coal Mines Regulation Act, 1887, with notes ; *cloth* 1 0

"JULIAN."

The Pillars of the Church: or the Gospels and Councils ... 0 6

Natural Reason versus Divine Revelation. An Appeal for Freethought. Edited by Robert Lewins, M.D. 0 6

KNOX, W. M.

Man's Alleged Spiritual Nature 0 2

LAIRD, JAMES L.

(Translated by) The Darwinian Theory, and the Law of the Migration of Organisms. From the German of Moritz Wagner, Honorary Professor at the Ludwig Maximilian University of Munich, and Member Extraordinary of the Royal Bavarian Academy of Sciences 1 0

LEWINS, ROBERT, M.D.

Life and Mind: on the Basis of Modern Medicine; *cloth* ... 1 0

Humanism versus Theism 0 6

Auto-Centricism; or the Brain-Theory of Life and Mind ... 0 6

LENNSTRAND, VICTOR.

The God Idea. A Lecture; for delivering which the author was sentenced to six month's imprisonment. Translated from the Swedish. With an introduction by J. M. Wheeler 0 2

MAJOR F——

The Agonies of Hanging. By one who was cut down from the Gallows 0 3

MASSEY GERALD.

Lectures (privately printed).

The Historical Jesus and the Mythical Christ 0 6

Paul as a Gnostic Opponent, not the Apostle of Historic Christianity 0 6

The Logia of the Lord; or the Pre-Christian sayings abscribed to Jesus the Christ 0 6

The Devil of Darkness, or Evil in the Light of Evolution ... 0 6

Man in search of his Soul and how he Found it 0 6

The Seven Souls of Man and the Culmination in Christ ... 0 6

Gnostic and Historic Christianity 0 6

Luniolatry, Ancient and Modern 0 6

The Hebrew and other Creations 0 6

The Coming Religion 0 6

"MATERIALIST."

A Reply to Cardinal Manning's Essay on "The Relation of Will to Thought" 0 3

MEREDITH, EVAN POWELL.

The Prophet of Nazareth... ... ... 7 6

MILL, JOHN STUART.

On Blasphemy; A reprint of an Article contributed to the "Westminster Review" for July, 1824, occasioned by the Prosecution of Richard Carlile 0 2

MITCHELL, LOGAN.

Religion in the Heavens; or Mythology Unveiled; *cloth* ... 2 6

MOSS, A. B.

Christianity a Degrading Religion 0 1
Natural Man 0 1
Delusions of Theology 0 1
Nature and the Gods 0 1
Man and the Lower Animals 0 1
Bible Saints and Sinners. Parts I., II., and III., each ... 0 1
The Bible and Evolution: with a Preface by Dr. H. J. Hardwicke; paper boards, 1/-, *cloth* 2 6

MOZARK ZAZ.

Holy Ghost's Arithmetic 0 1

NAEWIGER, G. E. CONRAD.

God is Love; Is it true? 0 2

NEVINS, W. P.

Development versus Fossilized Christianity 0 6

NORDAU, MAX.

The Conventional Lies of our Civilisation. Contents: The Religious Lie, The Lie of Monarchy and Aristocracy, The Political Lie, The Economic Lie, The Matrimonial Lie, etc. Published in America at one dollar, 364 pp. ... 3 0

Paradoxes. Contents: Optimism and Pessimism, Majority and Minority, Natural History of Love, Gratitude, The Psycho-Physiology of Genius and Talent, A Glance into the Future, etc. Published in America at one dollar, 377 pp. 3 0

"OXONIENSIS."

	s.	d.
Early Marriage and Late Parentage: the only solution of the social problem	0	2

PAINE, THOMAS.

Age of Reason	1	0
Rights of Man. *Cloth*, 2/-	1	0
Miscellaneous Works	1	0
Common Sense	0	6
Complete Theological Works: *cloth*	2	6

PORTRAITS and PHOTOGRAPHS.

A Fine Chromo-Lithographic Portrait of the late Mr. C. Bradlaugh, suitable for framing. Post free in Lett's protecting case	0	8
Cabinet Photograph by Elliott and Fry, ...	2	0
ditto by Amey	1	6
Large Lithograph Portrait of Col. Robert G. Ingersoll. A fine portrait of the great orator. Free by parcel post ...	0	9
Cabinet Photograph	1	0
Imperial Photograph of G. W. Foote, for framing	3	0
Cabinet ditto	1	0
Cabinet Photograph of Mrs. Besant	1	6
Cabinet Photograph of Robert Forder	1	0

READE, WINWOOD.

The Martyrdom of Man	7	6

RENAN, ERNEST.

Life of Jesus, *cloth*	1	6
The Apostles, *cloth*	1	6
Saint Paul, *cloth*	1	6
The Anti-Christ, *cloth*	1	6
The Gospels, *cloth*	1	6
The Christian Church, *cloth*	1	6
Marcus Aurelius, *cloth*	1	6
The Song of Songs, or Song of Solomon, *cloth*	1	6
The Book of Job, *cloth*	1	6
Leaders of Christian and Anti-Christian Thought, *cloth* ...	1	6

ROBERTSON, J. M.

Modern Humanists	2	6
The Fallacy of Saving	2	6

"SALADIN."

	s.	d.
Roses and Rue	3	0
The Whirlwind, Sown and Reaped: a tale of a Soul Saved ...	0	6
Isaure and other Poems	2	0
Lays of Romance and Chivalry; *cloth*	2	0
Cheap Edition, paper covers	1	0
God and his Book; 380 pp., *cloth*	3	0
Woman: her Glory, her Shame, and her God; two vols. ...	5	0
The Confessional: Romish and Anglican. An Exposure ...	1	0
Christianity and the Slave Trade	1	0
Did Jesus Christ Rise from the Dead?	0	6
A Visit to Mr. Spurgeon's Tabernacle	0	1
Robert Burns; was he a Freethinker?	0	1
Witchcraft in Christian Countries	0	2
Christian Persecution	0	1
The Divine Interpretation of Scripture	0	1
The Crusades	0	1
The Flagellants	0	1
Religious Education. Parts I., II., and III., each	0	1
The Inquisition. Parts I., and II.	0	1
Cabinet Portrait	1	0
A Fearful Flogging. By one who endured it. Printed from MSS. in the hands of Saladin	0	3
The New Crusades: a brilliant Satire on the Salvation Army. Published at 1/-, [postage, 2d.]	0	4

SALADIN & JOSEPH TAYLOR.

Why I am an Agnostic. A Manual of Agnosticism; *cloth* ... 1 6

SAMSON, Mrs. LOUISA.

Why Women should be Secularists 0 2

SAVILLE, W. C.

The Question of Questions. Christianity, what? which? where? 0 1

SHAW, GEORGE BERNARD.

Cashel Byron's Profession. A novel 1 0

SHELLEY, PERCY BYSSHE

On Blasphemy; being his Letter to Lord Ellenborough occasioned by the sentence he passed on Mr. D. I. Eaton as publisher of the third part of Paine's Age of Reason 0 1

SHORE, THOMAS.

Men *versus* Machinery. Suggestive facts and figures urging national control of national powers of production. With preface by H. H. Sparling 0 2

SOCIALISM.

Four nights' Debate between Annie Besant and G. W. Foote: subject, "Is Socialism Sound?" *cloth*, superior paper, 2/- 1 0
Debate between C. Bradlaugh and H. Hyndman; subject, "Will Socialism Benefit the English People?"... ... 0 3
Modern Socialism, by Mrs. Besant 0 6
Mrs. Besant's Socialism, by W. P. Ball. A reply to Mrs. Besant's "Modern Socialism" 0 3
The Curse of Capital, By Dr. E. B. Aveling 0 1
Socialism a Curse, by "Humanitas" 0 3
Socialism; its Fallacies and Dangers, by C. Bradlaugh ... 0 2
For and Against, by A. Besant and C. Bradlaugh 0 4
Debate on Socialism between C. Bradlaugh and E. Belfort Bax 0 6
Collected Essays on Socialism, by Annie Besant 2 6

STANDRING, GEORGE.

The People's History of the English Aristocracy 1 0
Court Flunkeys: their Work and Wages 0 1
Does Royalty Pay? 0 1
Life of C. Bradlaugh, with portrait and autograph 0 1
Life of Col. R. G. Ingersoll, with portrait and autograph ... 0 1

STRANGE, T. LUMISDEN.

Gospel Contradictions, arranged in the form of a dialogue ... 0 1
Why I Became and Why I ceased to be a Christian 0 2

STRAUSS, DAVID FREDERICK.

The Old Faith and the New. Two vols. in one, with portrait, *cloth*, gilt lettered 7 6

STRICKLAND, W. W., Trin. Coll., Cambridge.

Seven Poems; *cloth* 2 0

SYMES, JOSEPH.

Blows at the Bible. Six numbers in wrapper; containing The Sermon on the Mount, How a Fairy was Transformed, Jumping Comments on Genesis I., II, and III. 0 6

TAYLOR, Rev. ROBERT, B.A.

The Diegesis 3 6
Raising the Devil... ... ... 0 2

THOMPSON, ALFRED.

Magic and Mystery. All about the Secret and Wonderful; *cloth* 2 0

"VERITAS."

Republicanism: What does it mean? 0 2

VOLNEY, M.

The Ruins: A Survey of the Revolutions of Empires; *cloth* 2 0
Lectures on History 0 6

VOLTAIRE, M. DE.

The Philosophical Dictionary: two vols. 8 0
Philosophical Tales and Romances 2 6
Important Examination of the Holy Scriptures 0 4

"VULCAN."

True Democracy 0 1

WHEELER, J. M.

Frauds and Follies of the Early Christian Fathers 0 6
A Biographical Dictionary of Freethinkers of all Ages and Nations. Parts I. to XI., in wrapper, each 0 6
Handsomely bound in cloth 7 6
The Christian Doctrine of Hell 0 2
Letters from Heaven 0 1
Letters from Hell... ... ... 0 1
Freethought Readings and Secular Songs (compiled by J. M. Wheeler). Parts I. to V., each 0 6
In one volume, *cloth* 2 6

WINDEYER, Mr. JUSTICE.

Is Limitation of the Family Immoral? A Judgment on Annie Besant's "Law of Population," delivered in the Supreme Court of New South Wales, by Mr. Justice Windeyer, Senior Puisne Judge ... ...

WYSTYN, ADYN.

In Darkest Edinburgh: A Plea 0 3

LIST B.

SPECIAL LIST OF REMAINDERS.

The Prices quoted are nett, and orders must be accompanied by cost of postage. Where no postage is mentioned, the goods go by rail or carrier at cost of purchaser.

ANONYMOUS.

The Gospel History and Doctrinal Teachings Critically Examined. By the author of "Mankind, their Origin and Destiny." (An invaluable work to the Freethinker, showing how, when, and where the Canon of the New Testament was formed.) Published at 10/6. Reduced to [postage, 4½d.]... ... ... 2 6

BALE, G. G. P.,

Anatomy and Physiology of Man. Student's Edition, pub. at 10/6, [postage 4½d.]... ... ... 5 0
School Edition, pub. at 7/6, [postage 4½d.] 2 6

BESANT, ANNIE, Edited by

Our Corner. A monthly Freethought and Socialistic Magazine, 1883 to 1888. A few complete sets in 12 half yearly volumes, *cloth, gilt* 25 0

A few odd volumes of the above [postage, 4½d.] 1 6

CHALLICE, J., M.D.

Medical Advice to Mothers on the Management of Children in Health and Disease; limp cloth, 98 pp., [postage 1d.] 0 3

CONWAY, MONCURE D.

Liberty and Morality, post free 0 3
Human Sacrifices in England [postage, 1d.] 0 3
Republican Superstitions. Pub. at 7/6, [postage 3d.] ... 1 6

CURWEN, H.

A History of Booksellers, Old and New: Numerous Portraits and Illustrations. 8vo, 483 pp., [postage 4½d.]... ... 2 6

GEBLER, CARL Von.

Galileo Galilei. Demy 8vo, 356 pp., [postage 6d.] 4 0

GIBBON, EDWARD.

Decline and Fall of the Roman Empire. With Notes and Memoirs by Guizot. Containing 1310 pp., with complete Indices, and a portrait of Gibbon from a painting by Reynolds. In two vols., super royal 8vo. (pub. by Virtue and Co. at 36/-) 8 6

GILBERT, WILLIAM.

The City; an inquiry into the Corporation, its Livery Companies, and the Administration of their Charities and Endowments. *Cloth, gilt lettered,* published at 5/- [postage 4½d.] 1 0

GILES, Rev. Dr.

Hebrew, Christian, and Apostolic Records. In three vols. 1310 pp., published at 34/6 10

Apostolic Records, from the date of the Crucifixion to the middle of the second century. Pub. at 10/6. 438 pp. [postage, 6d.] 3 6

"One feels astonished that the man who wrote this book could remain a priest in the Church of England. To justify their existance, the young lions of the Christian Evidence Society ought certainly to attempt a reply to this remarkable work."—Extract from a letter from a Cambridge M.A.

HERSHON, PAUL ISAAC.

Genesis, with a Talmudical Commentary. With an introductory Essay on the Talmud by H. D. Spencer; *cloth gilt*, 560 pp., pub. at 10/6; [postage, 6d.] 2 0

HONE, WILLIAM.

The Apocryphal New Testament. Being all the Gospels and Epistles now extant, attributed to Jesus Christ, his Apostles and companions, not included in the new Testament. Royal 8vo., *cloth*, pub. at 5/-; [postage, 4½d.] 2 6

Ancient Mysteries Described. With engravings on copper and wood; very curious, pub. at 5/-; [postage 4½d.] ... 2 6

HUGHAN, SAMUEL.

Hereditary Peers and Hereditary Paupers: the two extremes of English Society. 152 pp., large 8vo, [postage, 3d.]

ILLINGWORTH, THOMAS.

Distribution Reform; The Remedy for Industrial Depression and for the Removal of many Social Evils. 180 pp., pub. at 1/-; [post free] 0 6

LOOG, HERMAN.

The Gospel of Nature: The Firmament (Astronomy). Crown 8vo, 148 pp., published at 2/6, [postage, 3d.] 0 9

MACCALL (WILLIAM).

National Missions: A series of Lectures. Contents.—I. Introductory, II. Egypt and Religion, III. Greece and Beauty, IV. Palestine and Faith, V. Rome and Force, VI. Arabia and Miracle, VII. Italy and Art, VIII. France and Manners, IX. Spain and Romance, X. Germany and Thought, XI. England and Science, etc., etc. Demy 8vo., Cloth, new, pp. 381, Published at 5/- [Postage 4½d.] 2 0

The Agents of Civilization: A series of Lectures. Contents. —The Hero, The Poet, The Priest, The Artist, The Prophet, The Philosopher, The Apostle, The Martyr, etc., etc. Crown 8vo, Cloth, new, pp. 118. Published at 2/6, [Postage 3d.] 1 0

The Newest Materialism. Sundry Papers on the Books of Mill, Comte, Bain, Spencer, Atkinson, and Feuerbach; *cloth*; pub. at 5/-; [postage, 3d.]... ... ... 1 0

MACKAY, W. R., M.A. (Translated by)

The Sophistes of Plato; a Dialogue on the True and False Teaching; with explanatory notes, and an introduction on Ancient and Modern Sophistry. Published at 5/-; [postage, 3d.] 1 0

"POPULATION ESSAYS."

By Dr. Allbutt, Mrs. Besant, Dr. Knowlton, and J. M. Robertson. About 200 pp., in one vol., *cloth*, [postage, 3d.] ... 3 0

PRIOR, H. M.

My Experience of the Catholic Apostolic Church. *Cloth*, Crown 8vo, published at 1/6, [postage, 2d.] 0 6

SCOTT, THOMAS.

English Life of Jesus; [postage, 4½d.] 2 6

SHAKESPEARE, W.

The Play of Hamlet. Splendidly illustrated, 70 pp. in wrapper; [postage, 1d.] 0 3

SMART, B. H.

Pronouncing Dictionary, Walker remodelled, with a key to the pronunciation of Greek, Latin, and Scripture names, 700 pp., quite new, in cloth, pub. at 6s., the best pronouncing dictionary extant; [postage, 4½d.] 1 6

STRANGE, T. LUMISDEN.

Contribution to a Series of Controversial Writings. Cloth, crown 8vo., about 200 pp., published at 3/-, [postage, 3d.] 1 6

What is Christianity? An Historical Sketch, illustrated, with a Chart. Crown 8vo, *cloth*, published at 1/6: [postage, 2d.] 1 0

TAYLOR, Rev. ROBERT, B.A.

The Devil's Pulpit; two vols. cloth. Pub. at 8/- 4 0

For this latter work the author was sentenced to two years' imprisonment and a heavy fine for blasphemy.

TENNANT, CHARLES.

The People's Blue Book: Taxation as it is, and as it should be. Revised and enlarged, with a supplementary chapter on Ireland, 966 pp. Post free, 1/6 ... ... 1 0

TRELAWNEY, EDWARD JOHN.

Records of Shelley, Byron, and the Author. New Edition, with two portraits. Cloth, crown 8vo., 312 pp., [postage, 4½d.] 4 0

WATSON, Rev. J. S., M.A.

Biographies of John Wilkes and William Cobbett, with steel engravings. Good index, 410 pp., [postage, 4½d.] ... 2 6

WILLIS, R. M.D.

Servetus and Calvin. With splendid portraits of Servetus and Calvin. Demy 8vo, 542 pp., pub. at 16/-, [postage, 6d.] 4 0

Published by

Facsimile Publisher
Ashok Vihar, Delhi-110052 (India)
Website: www.facsimilepublisher.com

Distributed by

Gyan Books Pvt. Ltd.
5, Ansari Road, Daryaganj, New Delhi-110002 (India)
E-mail: books@gyanbooks.com, Website: www.gyanbooks.com

2 222000 009717